THE MARKETING PLAN PROJECT MANUAL

WILLIAM QUAIN, PH.D.

COLLEGE OF BUSINESS ADMINISTRATION
THE UNIVERSITY OF CENTRAL FLORIDA

GLEN R. JARBOE, PH.D.

DEPARTMENT OF MARKETING
THE UNIVERSITY OF TEXAS AT ARLINGTON

WEST PUBLISHING COMPANY
MINNEAPOLIS/ST. PAUL   NEW YORK   LOS ANGELES   SAN FRANCISCO

Production, Prepress, Printing and Binding by West Publishing Company.

COPYRIGHT © 1993 by   WEST PUBLISHING CO.
610 Opperman Drive
P.O. Box 64526
St. Paul, MN 55164–0526

ISBN 0–314–01341–5

CONTENTS

PREFACE

This manual has been written to help you conduct a student marketing plan project. We have used projects of this type in teaching marketing planning for many years. On many occasions, our students have said they found the marketing project to be one of their most rewarding educational experiences.

This manual is designed to guide you in a step-by-step manner through a marketing plan project. Your project will help you develop and refine a number of skills that can only be acquired by actually writing a marketing plan. You will find that the material in this manual will answer many detailed questions that students encounter while developing their project. Often, this type of detail is simply not covered in a marketing textbook. This manual takes a specific how-to-do-it approach. However, every student plan is different and the purpose of the material presented in this manual is to encourage, not to restrain, your creativity.

The manual has been designed around an example of a typical student project. The first few chapters orient you to the project and provide some useful information about finding and choosing a client to work with. In Chapter Three, you will meet Ms. Amanda Chelsea. She is the manager of Haggerty's, a restaurant and bar located in Orlando, Florida. Haggerty's provides an example of a marketing plan that will be used throughout this manual. In Chapter Four, you will learn how to present information effectively using graphs, charts, and tables.

In Chapter Five, you will view a detailed outline for a three-part marketing plan. To complete this project, all you will have to do is fill in the outline to this plan. Chapters Six, Seven, and Eight are the real meat of this project. You will undertake a series of exercises that are designed to help you develop the information necessary to complete the plan. Finally, in Chapter Nine, you will find some more advanced methods for analyzing the profitability of market plans.

We believe that you will find this project to be a genuinely rewarding, educational experience. You will not only be acquiring and applying new skills, but you will be challenged to think like a marketer. You will also experience firsthand the excitement of a career in marketing, as a supplier or as a user of marketing plans.

William Quain
The University of Central Florida
November, 1992

Glen Jarboe
The University of Texas at Arlington
November, 1992

ACKNOWLEDGMENTS

The authors wish to extend special thanks to the following people:

Cheryl Pinger, for manuscript preparation;
Jeanne Quain, for editing and review;
Ed Suchora, for computer support;
Barry Render, for his writing expertise;
Bill Zikmund, Craig Kelley, and W.R. Brown, for insightful review and recommendations; and
Jessica Evans, for quiet support.

For
Diane, John, Maliz, Joan, Cindy, and Jeannine

CHAPTER ONE
THE MARKETING PLAN PROJECT

INTRODUCTION

This manual has been written to help guide you through a marketing plan project. The entire outline for a detailed marketing plan is provided in Chapter Five. It will be your job to obtain the information necessary to fill in the outline and to complete the plan. This manual is intended to answer many of the questions that are typically encountered in translating the concepts and ideas you have learned into practical application. While it is not likely to answer all your questions, it will discuss most of the difficulties that students have encountered in conducting projects of this type.

Although this manual contains a complete, step-by-step outline for the marketing plan, you will still need to apply creativity and originality to the task. You will encounter many questions to which there is no single, correct answer. No two student groups will approach the planning process in exactly the same way. Every plan is unique. However, you and your classmates, working on different projects, may encounter many of the same situations.

OVERVIEW OF THE PROJECT

You will be completing an entire marketing plan project from start to finish. Such a project involves identifying target markets, examining past and present company performance, creating strategies and selling ideas, and finally, writing action plans.

1

Throughout this project, your instructor will serve as an advisor to answer questions not covered in this manual. However, this is *your* project. All of the important steps will be carried out by you and your group. In effect, your team may be thought of as a group of student consultants and, throughout the term, you will be working for a "client," some organization to which you believe you can be of assistance. Your instructor will probably allow you to develop your own list of potential clients and select one of them to work with. If you have difficulty coming up with a client, your instructor may have some ideas. Business people often contact universities with ideas for student projects, and your instructor may know of some. However, the authors' experience has been that most student groups can come up with several excellent project ideas without much prompting.

In effect, your student group becomes a small marketing company. You will gain an appreciation for the value and conduct of marketing, and develop some feeling about this field as a potential career opportunity. While this process will represent a lot of hard work, students often report that it is one of their most satisfying experiences in business school.

BENEFITS TO BE GAINED

Practical Experience. The most obvious benefit to be gained from conducting this project is the practical experience you will acquire. Many students find that they do not truly understand the concepts and ideas they learn in the classroom until they are required to apply them in an actual situation. Such a fundamental concept as market segmentation takes on a new meaning when you are required to carefully identify, define, and measure the characteristics of some important customer group(s).

Satisfaction of Producing a Product. Students often find considerable satisfaction in doing the marketing plan project. This exercise will involve you from start to finish in solving a practical problem. At this point, it may be hard for you to imagine what the final product will be like. However, if your feelings are similar those of other students, you will be proud to see what you have done when it is finished. The final report of your project will truly be a product that you and your group have created.

Application of Skills. This project will require you to apply a variety of skills. Some of these skills may be entirely new, such as applying customer segment information into a computer. Others may be skills that you began to acquire in other classes but have not applied to marketing problems, for example, using the graphics capabilities of a spreadsheet program to prepare graphs or bar charts.

Exposure to a Professional Experience. You may find that this project is as close as you will come during your college career to experiencing the things that professionals regularly encounter. A single course in marketing is not going to make you a professional marketing strategist. However, by completing this project in a step-by-step manner, you will gain valuable professional experience. You will find that the lessons learned in preparing a marketing plan can be applied to many sources of business endeavors.

You will find that the lessons learned in preparing a marketing plan can be applied to many sources of business endeavors.

In addition, you may find your final report very useful when you begin looking for a career. Most recruiters, while they may not ask for it, are pleased to see examples of your college work. Your transcript tells them something about the things that you *know* as a result of the university experience. Projects of this type help them to evaluate the things that you can *do*.

DIFFICULTY OF WORKING WITH OTHERS

While the benefits of doing this project may be substantial, do not underestimate its difficulty. While some people are naturally attracted to working on projects as part of a group, others take a more independent approach to their education. A project of this type will require you to work with and depend upon others, some of whom may not share your level of knowledge and enthusiasm. This is an excellent opportunity to experience the dynamics of working as part of a team.

FORMING A PROJECT GROUP

Your instructor may simply assign you to a project group without regard to your preferences. However, it is likely that he or she may allow you some discretion in deciding with whom you want to work. Typically, a group size of five to seven works well. In order to allow you to focus on the important tasks of market planning, your instructor may expect each student to participate fully in all aspects of the project. If the group is too small, the task of writing a marketing plan can be overwhelming. However, with too many students, the difficulty of working in such a large group can ruin the creative process.

There are a number of things that you might consider in forming a project group.

1. It would be desirable to have more than one person who has some experience with a word processor. Preferably they would both use the same program, such as WORD-PERFECT, MICROSOFT WORD, or WORDSTAR.

   (Authors' Note: This entire manual was prepared with WORDPERFECT 5.1 using Times Roman and Helvetica fonts.)

2. It would also be desirable to have one or two people who enjoy using the computer. Spreadsheet programs and graphics programs will increase your ability to use marketing data and enhance your presentation.

3. It is easier for students with similar class schedules to get together for meetings. Some groups may try to include members who live close to school. In a large

metropolitan area, students who live in close proximity to each other might want to get together.

4. Some people naturally seek others with whom they feel they can work compatibly, perhaps based upon a previous group experience in another class. This may be an important factor so long as consideration is given to the skills mentioned above.

Appendix 1A contains a brief information sheet that your instructor may ask you to turn in. If some people desire to form their own work group, the sheets should be turned in together. This information sheet will help the instructor to check on the skills inventory in each group or to form groups of students who do not express any membership preferences.

GROUP ORGANIZATION AND LEADERSHIP

On the day when group assignments are made, your instructor may allow you to use the last few minutes of the class period to get together, exchange phone numbers, and plan for your first meeting. (The form contained in Appendix 1B provides you a place to record team names, phone numbers, meeting times, etc.) Prior to your first meeting, every member of the group should review this manual to get an idea of what will be involved in the project. At least the first three chapters should be read entirely. Reading the entire project manual would be even more desirable. (It isn't all that long, you are going to have to do it sooner or later, and it will give you a better idea of what the course and project are about.)

At your first meeting you should appoint (or elect) a team leader and give his or her name to the instructor. It will be up to the group to decide on the limits of this person's authority. Optimally, all group decisions will be made by consensus, and this person will simply be the instructor's primary point of contact with the group. However, occasional disputes may arise that will have to be resolved. The group might decide that all such questions will be voted on, or perhaps the group leader will be allowed to resolve them.

One of the most difficult aspects of group projects is getting the entire group together on short notice. It may be desirable to establish a regularly scheduled weekly meeting, for instance, Wednesday afternoon at 3:00 as well as one or two alternative meeting times. (Some project activities require group meetings more than once a week.) The group (or team leader) may occasionally decide to cancel a weekly meeting if it is not needed. Having a preplanned, regular meeting time will allow each group member to schedule other activities around the expected time.

Each member of the group should plan to attend all regularly scheduled meetings. This will help to maintain everyone's involvement. It will also ensure that the benefits of group rather than individual efforts are realized. This is especially important in the early stages of the Situation Analysis. Also, at the end of each meeting, the activities for the next group meeting should be discussed so that all group members will be prepared.

Some groups try to overcompartmentalize this project. For instance, they will assign one group member to write one section of the project, and then try to integrate all the sections together. While this may be a useful way to prepare for meetings, it will cause serious problems when developing your final project. A marketing plan is a three-step process. Each part of the plan builds upon the part that precedes it. While it is possible to assign action plans to various members of the group, the entire project must be integrated thoroughly.

TEAM EVALUATION

At the end of the term, your instructor may ask you to evaluate the contribution of the members of your group to the project. The instructor may provide you a form or suggest that you use the one contained in Appendix 1C. The form in the appendix requests that you evaluate only the other members of your group. However, you may use the comments section to point out various aspects of your own performance. Often, the instructor will choose to assign an overall grade to the group project and then give separate grades to each individual group member. This would reward some team members for their extra hard work and creativity.

APPENDIX 1A
STUDENT BACKGROUND FORM

NAME _____   Team _____

CLASSIFICATION   Freshman   Sophomore   Junior   Senior   Graduate

MAJOR   Marketing   Other Business   Other

RESIDENCE   On Campus   Near Campus   Far from Campus

EMPLOYMENT   None   Part-Time   Full-Time

ARE MOST OF YOUR CLASSES   Day   Night

        FOUNDATION COURSES COMPLETED

	Day	Night
Consumer Behavior	No	Yes
Psychology	No	Yes
Business Report Writing	No	Yes
Principles of Marketing	No	Yes
Marketing Strategy	No	Yes
Information Systems/Management Science	No	Yes
At least one semester of Statistics	No	Yes
OTHER_____ . .	No	Yes
OTHER_____ . .	No	Yes

        COMPUTER SKILLS

	Day	Night
Word Processing	No	Yes
Spreadsheets	No	Yes
Graphics Programs	No	Yes
Other_____	No	Yes
Other_____	No	Yes

Have you used a personal computer and modem to
communicate with campus computers? . . . .   No   Yes

Have you completed a major business project in
any other course? . . . .   No   Yes

Other Information Desired by the Instructor:

_____

_____

_____

APPENDIX 1B
GROUP INFORMATION SHEET

YOUR NAME _____ Team _____

MEETING TIMES:	DAY	TIME	PLACE
Regular Meeting	_____	_____	_____
Alternate # 1	_____	_____	_____
Alternate # 2	_____	_____	_____

GROUP COMPOSITION:

TEAM MEMBER_____ Phone_____

Special Skills _____

TEAM MEMBER_____ Phone_____

Special Skills _____

TEAM MEMBER_____ Phone_____

Special Skills _____

TEAM MEMBER_____ Phone_____

Special Skills _____

TEAM MEMBER_____ Phone_____

Special Skills _____

TEAM MEMBER_____ Phone_____

Special Skills _____

TEAM MEMBER_____ Phone_____

Special Skills _____

APPENDIX 1C
PEER EVALUATION

The purpose of this form is to allow you to evaluate the relative contribution of the members of your group to the project you have performed. Your instructor may ask you to assign a score to the overall contribution of each team member, or she/he may ask you to evaluate individual areas as well as the overall contribution. In making your evaluation, you should divide 100 points among the members of the group, other than yourself. Thus, the total in each column should be 100. You will not evaluate yourself. However, you may use the "Comments" space at the bottom of the form, as well as the back, to mention specific aspects of your performance, or to provide written comments about the team members.

TEAM MEMBERS	SPECIAL AREAS			OVERALL CON-TRIBUTION
	CONCEPTU-ALIZATION	PROJECT EXECUTION	OTHER	
Your Name:	DO NOT EVALUATE YOURSELF			------ ------
Other Team Members:	------	------	-------	------
TOTAL	100	100	100	100

COMMENTS:

11

CHAPTER TWO
THE VALUE OF PLANNING

OVERVIEW

Organizations and individuals can both benefit from a plan. Plans provide direction, measurability, and energy for an organization. As a student, you operate within some form of plan. You probably have an expected graduation date and some expectations for life after college. However, without a plan for completing your degree, you will not likely meet your goals.

Plans are a framework for operations. They are the day-to-day guides for completing work and assessing progress. When we plan, we recognize the importance of today's activities in reaching tomorrow's goals.

Businesses could not exist without plans. Resources must be allocated, products designed, and goals met. Even if they are not written down, plans are in effect for all successful businesses. To be most effective, however, a company must have written plans.

THE PLANNING PROCESS

In marketing, we use a term called "Problem Recognition." Consumers look for a new product or attempt to replenish the supply of an old product when they have problem recognition. We often use the example of someone who is making a bologna sandwich to illustrate this concept.

If you are hungry, you might go to the refrigerator to make a bologna sandwich. You take out two pieces of bologna, spread mustard on them, put some lettuce and tomato on top and then go to the pantry for some bread. When you get to the pantry, you discover that there is no bread. You recognize that a problem exists. Marketers often describe this as "Recognizing that a desired state is different than the actual state." Now you set about solving the problem.

The first step is to set objectives. You want to find two pieces of bread. Secondly, you establish a plan. With bologna in hand, you then execute the plan by driving your car to the store, purchasing bread, bringing it home, and then transferring the lunchmeat to the bread. Next, you take out a glass, put some chocolate syrup into it and then go to the refrigerator; to discover that you are out of milk!

Planning usually occurs when a problem is recognized. The organization or individual is at point A and wishes to go to point B. Plans establish the routine for getting there. However, as our lunchtime example demonstrates, plans cannot operate within a vacuum. It is likely that one plan can easily be interrelated with others. It would have been a lot simpler to plan the whole meal, establishing desired outcomes and then gathering all the resources necessary to meet the expectations.

There are several basic steps to the planning process:

1.   Totally evaluate the current situation
2.   Set goals and objectives
3.   Establish strategies for resource allocation
4.   Create specific steps for reaching the goals
5.   Evaluate success or failure

Market planning utilizes these five steps. You will be amazed at how simple it is to train yourself to plan.

THE BENEFITS OF PLANNING

Planning should be systematic. That is, the steps taken to prepare plans should be repeated each time you plan. This reduces the chance of making the same mistake more than once. We can't eliminate mistakes, but we can make fewer errors if we repeat our positive actions and don't repeat the negative ones.

Managers make decisions every day. Some of these decisions will work out well, while others won't. When we plan, we write down both the decisions and the reasons for making those decisions. We can later review the outcome of these decisions. If the outcomes were positive, we can fully expect to repeat them, because by following the plan, we can implement them in exactly the same way. Without a written plan, it is necessary to rely on human memory.

Here is a list of some benefits to planning:

1.   Decision making is reduced. If our original decision is correct, we simply repeat it.

2.   Objectives are clearly stated. We know <u>when</u> the job is complete and <u>how</u> we performed. This increases job satisfaction by reducing uncertainty.

3.   When plans are prepared in advance, everyone has a chance for input. Costly duplication or oversights might be avoided.

4.   Plans can be changed or revised as new information becomes available.

5.   Businesses can evaluate the probability of meeting goals before they are attempted.

6.   Factors outside the business are considered. These could include competition, legal and political changes or economic disruptions.

7.   The process of planning should involve the entire organization. This increases the commitment to the plan.

Unfortunately, plan writing is often something that management feels should be done, but not really implemented. So the task of writing a plan is assigned to some luckless individual. He or she spends hours gathering information, preparing the document, and even presenting it at meetings. It is then put into a drawer and revised the next year.

Plan writing is a participative effort. It should not just be a top down memorandum. Input should be solicited from all of the operational and staff departments within the organization. Production, accounting, marketing, finance, and even R&D should contribute to the plan. In fact, each of these departments should have their own plans. The departmental plans should compliment and augment the overall goals and objectives of the organization.

Marketing plans should, of course, be written by the marketing department. The marketing department will consult with the other functional areas of the company. Although the plan document may actually be prepared by middle management personnel, the marketing plan should have the full support and input of the Marketing Director. This person, in turn, should have the plan approved by the executive board.

You don't need to be a marketing whiz with 20 years of experience to write a marketing plan, however. As you are about to discover, <u>you</u> can write a very credible marketing plan. Of course, experience is helpful. You will improve each time you prepare a plan.

In order to prepare you for the planning process, we have given you an exercise to complete. Appendix 2A contains a form for completing your personal plan. You cannot write plans for others until you first write one for yourself. Your instructor may ask you to complete this exercise and submit it as a homework assignment.

PLANNING AND THE CORPORATE CULTURE

Planning comes naturally to most corporations. Controlling the operations of a variety of departments can only be accomplished under the auspices of a plan. Corporations often have steering committees. These are groups of upper level managers who determine policy and strategy. Departments and business units then devise plans to implement the strategies.

If you go to work for a large company, you will be working for their plan. Unfortunately, in some companies, the people at the lower levels are often unaware of the overall plan. This can lead to fragmentation of the work effort. Many companies now have internal marketing campaigns that "sell" the plan to their own employees. This is especially important in a service company whose lower level employees are in direct contact with the customer.

In a corporation, there will usually be frequent meetings to update and evaluate the plan performance. Each unit will determine its contribution to the overall effort. As an employee of a large corporation, you will be judged on your ability to fulfill the plan's requirements for your position.

PLANNING AND SMALL BUSINESSES

Many small businesses operate in the absence of a formal plan. The owner of the company may also be one of the few employees. It may be less difficult to coordinate the various functions of the business. Production people and marketers may talk to each other daily. The accountants could have desks next to the sales staff. Still, there should be a written plan.

It is easy to lose sight of long-term goals when there are crises everyday. The Mission Statement might be forgotten when two key employees call in sick. Indeed, it might be necessary to go into an "emergency mode" to take care of a critical situation.

However, the presence of a plan, even in a small business, provides stability and direction. When the crisis has passed, the company can immediately resume its pursuit of the required objectives.

It is likely that the companies you use for this project will be small businesses. Be patient with them. Your plan can be a great benefit to them. They, in turn, can provide you with valuable lessons about customer issues, entrepreneurship, and business management. Nobody knows their customers better than a small business operator.

THE THREE PARTS OF A MARKETING PLAN

A marketing plan consists of three basic parts. They are:

1. The Situation Analysis
2. The Strategy
3. Action Plans

These three sections provide a fundamental flow of information. A brief description of each section follows.

Situation Analysis. This section examines the organization as it exists now. If a marketing plan was done last year, it is reviewed here. The Situation Analysis is a detailed description of the company's marketing effort. Price, Product, Distribution, and Promotion are reviewed. Environmental scanning is done to ascertain the effects of external variables, and the current markets are scrutinized. It is a snapshot of the company.

Strategy. Broad statements of direction are made. Goals are set and the individual strategies for each of the marketing mix variables are created.

Action Plans. These are the blueprints for success. Each Action Plan describes very specific activities. Advertising campaigns, product changes, sales trips, trade shows, and other marketing mix activities all have their own Action Plans. Each Action Plan has a cost estimate.

Chapter 5 contains a complete outline of the Three-Part Marketing Plan.

APPENDIX 2A
YOUR PERSONAL PLAN

You should have a plan for graduating and beginning a career. Use the form below to begin your personal plan.

I.   Goals And Objectives

Degree sought _____   I will graduate by _____

Special skills that you will develop before graduation, e.g., computer graphics, business writing, interviewing skills, etc.

1.   _____

2.   _____

3.   _____

4.   _____

5.   _____

Describe, in detail, what your life will be like five years after graduation - your job, salary, location, family status, etc.

_____

_____

_____

_____

II.   Plans

List the courses you still need to take in order to graduate, the semester in which you will take them, and the grade you intend to receive in each. USE A SEPARATE SHEET FOR ADDITIONAL ROOM IF NECESSARY.

Course Title	Semester	Grade
_____	_____	_____
_____	_____	_____
_____	_____	_____
_____	_____	_____

Course Title	Semester	Grade
_____	_____	_____
_____	_____	_____
_____	_____	_____
_____	_____	_____
_____	_____	_____
_____	_____	_____

Describe some of the specific steps that you will take to achieve your five year goals. For example, if you want to make $40,000 per year, what steps will you take to achieve this? Be both specific and brief. USE A SEPARATE SHEET FOR ADDITIONAL ROOM IF NECESSARY.

_____

_____

_____

_____

_____

III.   Evaluation

Now, evaluate your current progress toward your goals. Is it

_____ Poor   _____ Satisfactory   _____ Excellent

Also, provide a brief assessment of the objectives themselves. Do you feel that they are realistic and attainable? Can you easily reach them or will they be very difficult to attain?

_____

_____

_____

_____

_____

CHAPTER THREE
WORKING WITH A CLIENT

INTRODUCTION

Your first assignment involves the submission of one or more project ideas to your instructor. Your instructor will try to help you choose the most interesting and/or practical project. You should select a company that has the following factors associated with it:

1.   The company you select should already be in business.

2.   The company should be located near your College or University.

3.   Select a small- to medium-sized company.

4.   Select a company whose products or services interest you.

5.   It is best to select a company or organization whose products or services you are familiar with.

In your first group meeting, you should probably try to come up with a list of possible "clients." Any organization that has a group of customers to serve is a candidate. There will probably be several people in your group who own or work in a business, or know someone who does. If you are interested in working with a business, it is probably best to stick with a small one. While a large company may admire your enthusiasm, it is likely that it has marketing resources of its own. The following is a list of potential clients to consider:

1.   Campus organizations such as sports teams.

2.   Local restaurants and bars, especially those located on campus.

3.   Small service companies, such as dry cleaners, banks or travel agencies.

4.   Small hotels or inns.

5.   Businesses that serve the student market, such as print shops, bookstores, and public transportation.

The more familiar you are with a company's products or services, the easier it will be for you to write the marketing plan. Remember, you will probably need at least a minimum amount of financial information from these companies. A small, student-oriented company is more likely to share this information with you.

Some groups prefer to work with an area business rather than a campus organization or company. Students sometimes feel that this type of project is closer to the "real world." Small businesses often do not have adequate budget for marketing. Some may be unaware of its potential benefits. Others may have made a subjective judgment that the value of developing a total marketing plan is not likely to exceed its costs. However, most managers who are concerned with satisfying their customers or increasing their revenues can intuitively see the value in obtaining additional information from outside sources. Given that this project will be offered at little or no charge, small businesses often make enthusiastic clients.

An excellent source for project ideas is the Small Business Development Center (SBDC) located on many campuses. This is a quasi-governmental organization that serves local, small business clients. The director of your SBDC is often happy to provide you with potential clients.

It may take two or more group meetings for your group to decide upon a project. The first meeting could involve a discussion of the interests of the various group members and a brainstorming session to generate a list of prospective clients. After meeting with the managers of some of these establishments, a second meeting can be held to decide on a project.

TIPS ON CHOOSING A TOPIC

Chapter Five will discuss the process of marketing planning. However, at this point, it will be useful for you to consider some possible complications that might increase the difficulty of completing your project.

1. Avoid companies with a large number of complex products. It may be difficult for you to obtain working information on all of the various subsegments that this company services.

2. It is easier to write a plan for a company with existing customers than it is to discover the boundaries of new segments. This is not to say that you won't suggest new segments for your client.

3. Well-established companies with proven track records for their products or services are often the best clients. It is easier to recommend adjustments to the marketing mix variables than to create a total new marketing environment.

4. Avoid products about which you have absolutely no knowledge. For example, it is likely that the members of a student group do not use luxury cars. While they may desire one after five to ten years of work, present experiences may be limited.

WORKING WITH A CLIENT

Remember, you should think of your project team as a group of marketing consultants working to provide a marketing plan to a client. The initial contact should probably be made by one or two group members. During this conversation, there are several things that you should make very clear:

1. The project will be performed by a group of student consultants taking an introductory or intermediate course in marketing. Your instructor may provide you some assistance by answering your questions and reviewing your work. However, his or her limited involvement will not ensure that you will not make mistakes, or that your project will be up to industry standards.

2. The project will involve primary and secondary data, and the group's ingenuity to create a marketing plan. If the client has something else in mind, such as a study of the industry rather than of the business, this would not meet your course requirements.

3. The project will not take a great deal of the client's time. His or her involvement could be limited to:

   a. One or two meetings of an hour or so in duration to gather background material about the client's organization, marketing strategies, information needs, and potential marketing decisions.

   b. Occasional phone calls or visits to report on the progress of the plan and/or to clear up areas of confusion.

   c. The review and approval of your Situation Analysis.

   d. Providing background data, such as industry trade publications or published research reports.

   e. Providing a *small* amount of financial data, such as costs associated with providing certain services or manufacturing products.

   f. *Stress to the client that while you will probably need some cost information, the client will not need to provide detailed financial statements for income figures.*

4. The project may deviate considerably from what might be provided by professional marketing organizations. Your experience is probably limited, and the amount of financial data you will gather will be less than would be provided to a personal consultant.

5. Because the project is not being conducted by professionals, the results should be interpreted with caution, especially if used as a basis for marketing strategy planning or decision making.

6. If you are not prepared to make a commitment to the client during this initial cold call, make sure that she or he understands that the choice of a client to work with will be made by your project group with the advice of your instructor. After this decision is made, you will notify him or her.

YOU ARE A MARKETING EXPERT

Perhaps one of the most attractive aspects of a career in marketing is that it forces an individual to become familiar with a variety of different areas of business. An account executive in a marketing company could, in a given year, study fifteen to twenty different products or services and be involved in different stages of many projects at the same time. Considering the diversity of so many different types of businesses, one might wonder how people could develop an expertise in every possible field. The answer is, they usually don't.

Rather, the capable marketer develops a feel for common problems and solutions without getting lost in the detail that often obscures these problems from management. The one area in which a good marketing consultant *does* become an expert is general marketing. The marketer develops an intuitive feel for marketing management and decision making as a process.

MANAGERIAL DECISION MAKING AND MARKETING PLANNING

Before discussing how the marketer can help the business manager, we will examine what managers do. The essence of management is decision making; managers make decisions with respect to the allocation of resources. Marketing managers deal with special kinds of business resources. These are the controllable marketing variables, usually referred to as the marketing mix. They may have been referred to in your Principles of Marketing textbook as "the four P's." In this manual, the marketing mix variables are referred to as "the three P's and a D." We call the marketing mix variables, "product, price, promotion, and distribution." Marketing managers try to allocate these resources in the most efficient manner by directing them towards specific market segments.

Any decision involves a choice from a set of alternatives. The existence of two or more alternatives, one of which is believed to be more desirable, is the basis for decision making. In evaluating the desirability of alternatives, the manager must attempt to predict the outcomes resulting from alternative choices. This can be especially difficult since these outcomes will not occur until sometime in the future, and they may be affected by a wide variety of factors that are out of the manager's control. Nevertheless, the manager must gather as much information as reasonably possible to make an accurate prediction of these outcomes.

The information that the manager will use to predict these outcomes could come from a variety of sources, such as his or her own background and experience, the internal records of the company, information purchased from syndicated data services, or library research. However, sometimes the information is simply not available from any source and must be gathered directly. Such is the case with primary research studies.

A very useful type of information involves consumer response. Below is a brief list of some of the types of consumer response questions that might be asked by a typical marketing manager:

1. How would my customers react if I raised or lowered my price by five percent? What if my competitors did the same?

2. What would have a more positive impact on my sales, a five percent price reduction or the addition of a more attractive product feature?

3.   How would my business be affected if I moved to a more desirable location?

4.   Should I increase my advertising budget? For each dollar of increased advertising, how much additional revenue would be generated?

5.   Should I add additional styles and colors to my product line?

Clearly the answers to questions such as these will affect the decisions of the manager. Even prior to conducting marketing research and writing a plan, the manager probably has tentative answers and strategies based upon his or her own background and experience. The manager also knows that there may be considerable costs incurred if his or her beliefs are wrong. Thus, marketing planning can substantially reduce the inherent risk in decision making. It can do this by providing the manager with an additional and valuable perspective, that of the actual consumer.

THE INITIAL MEETING WITH YOUR CLIENT

Using a managerial decision making perspective will help you in designing a project with a strong decision focus. Some people will feel naturally hesitant about their first meeting with a client. Most students will have taken only one or two marketing courses. It should not be surprising if many people in your group do not yet *feel* like experts.

Nevertheless, that may be just what your client expects. The client's willingness to cooperate may depend on the perception your team creates during the first meeting. Little need be said about the importance of appropriate attire and behavior. Beyond this, however, your client's perception of your professionalism will be affected strongly by your ability to ask intelligent questions. A good guideline is to focus on a few key areas:

1.   Understanding the business

2.   Market segmentation

3.   Existing marketing plans and strategies

4.   What the manger knows, thinks or assumes about issues in each of these areas

Throughout this project manual, we will use an example focused on a particular business, Haggerty's. Haggerty's is a restaurant and bar located in Orlando, Florida. Consider the following discussion between a group of student consultants and Ms. Amanda Chelsea, the manager of Haggerty's:

Student: Ms. Chelsea, our job as student consultants is to gather information about your customers, your business, and your competitors that might help you in developing better marketing plans and strategies. There will be no charge to you for doing this project. The purpose of this meeting is for us to become familiar with your business and to explore how we might be able to contribute. After this meeting, we will prepare a proposal outlining how we feel we can help you. We will send you a copy of the proposal and then arrange another meeting to discuss our ideas. You will, of course, have final approval of the project.

Ms. Chelsea: Fine, I've thought a lot about doing a marketing plan in the past. I've assumed it would be far too complicated for a small business like ours. However, your offer sounds too attractive to turn down.

Student: Perhaps a good way to start would be for you to tell us something about the background of your business.

Ms. Chelsea: Well, we opened this restaurant about five years ago. We have 250 seats in the dining room and 60 seats in the lounge. Our concept is to provide a fun, medium-priced environment for lunch and evening dining. Our waiters and waitresses are all young people, mostly college students. Our major objective is to provide consistently good food to our clientele. But we are selling more than just food. We are selling entertainment. We want people to have fun when they come to Haggerty's.

Student: Who do you consider to be your main competitors?

Ms. Chelsea: When we first opened our business, there weren't too many restaurants in this area. Now, as this area has grown, so has our competition. There are several excellent chain restaurants in the area, such as Bennigan's and Friday's. Additionally, there are four, privately owned establishments that we compete with. Finally, even fast food restaurants offer competition. While their food is not as good as ours, nor their service as complete, they are an alternative that our guests will sometimes choose when they just want to grab something.

Student: How do you think your establishment is different from the others you just mentioned?

Ms. Chelsea: Well, in terms of the fast food restaurants, we obviously offer more service, selection, and entertainment. However, it is often difficult to differentiate us from the chain restaurants. We like to think of ourselves as being less "commercialized." Our dining area is a little more intimate and our menu is innovative. We offer "pub grub." While we offer the traditional array of snacks and appetizers, our entrees are more complete. We have an excellent chef.

Student: Do you think that this image is apparent to your customers?

Ms. Chelsea: I know it is to some. We have a very loyal group of customers whose repeat business we value. However, our competitors also offer a good product, and I think that our promotional material has not always done a good job in stressing our differences.

Student: If people have a tough time differentiating between your restaurant and the chain restaurants, why do you think your customers come to Haggerty's?

Ms. Chelsea: Well, that's a good question. I suppose there are really two answers. First, our prices tend to be lower. Certainly, our bar prices are more in line with what our customers expect to pay. We also serve a lot of specials for entrees, which allows us to take advantage of some good price breaks that we like to pass on to our customers. Second, bars and restaurants have sort of an intangible quality. I think many of our customers just feel more at home here.

Student: Do your loyal customers eat at your competitors' restaurants?

Ms. Chelsea: Yes. One of the reasons that people dine out is so that they can have a change. I suppose our best customers are those who dine out two or three times a week. While we do offer specials and change our menu periodically, it would be impossible for us to provide them with the variety that they would need to eat here every time they dine out. I'm sure our competitors feel the same way.

Student: How do you set your prices?

Ms. Chelsea: We have a two-step process for establishing prices. First, we like to keep our cost of goods sold (food costs) at about 35-45% of the menu prices. Second, we adjust sale prices up or down to create featured items and to give our menu a range of prices. People like having a choice. I suppose we also set our prices by considering the pricing of our competitors.

Student: How about your target market? Do you think you attract the same types of customers as your competitors?

Ms. Chelsea: I think we're a little more family-oriented than our competitors. They seem to focus more on a young, singles crowd. We're interested more in the customer who wants a complete meal. We do run specials in the bar for happy hour, and this does attract a good clientele, but the majority of our business comes from couples and small families.

Student: Do you promote your business? Do you do any advertising?

Ms. Chelsea: Yes, we advertise in the local newspaper in the dining section. Also, we run some radio spots. Finally, we do some spot advertising of our special events.

Student: Are there any particular marketing ideas that you have been considering as a way of expanding your business?

Ms. Chelsea: We are considering several options. We've thought about doing outside catering from our special pub grub menu. Also, we would like to periodically hire bands or other entertainers to improve our bar business later in the evening. We have also just started an early bird special to attract customers to the dining room before 7:00.

Student: Well, Ms. Chelsea, you have given us good information about your business. Is there any other place that you can think of where we could get additional information about the restaurant industry?

Ms. Chelsea: Yes, definitely. I would suggest that you check with the local restaurant association. They have a wide range of statistics about the industry in general and restaurants in this area in particular. Also, they get all of the trade magazines.

Student: Do you keep old issues of the trade publications?

Ms. Chelsea: Yes I do, for awhile. I have a box full of them right behind my desk. Would you like to take them?

Student: That would be great. I'm sure that some of those magazines would be difficult to find in our campus library. Is there anything else you think we should know that we haven't asked about, some additional information that might be useful to you?

Ms. Chelsea: I would be really interested in finding out more about my competition and the customers they serve. In the last year or so I really haven't kept up with them. Also, I would really like to have a better idea of where we are going strategically. Is this something that your group can provide?

Student: Yes, that's all part of the market planning process. We will be happy to do our best to provide you with the documents that will really answer your questions and that can serve as a guide for the future.

Ms. Chelsea: That would be great. I look forward to working with the group. I know that any information or suggestions that you can make could be very helpful.

Looking back on the conversation, a number of questions should occur to you that were not asked. And, you should be able to see how a number of answers to the questions could have been explored in greater detail. However, this hypothetical conversation is typical. During the brief discussion, the group encouraged Ms. Chelsea to talk about the market segment she was serving and market segments in which she might not be doing well. Characteristics of her product mix were explored. Her pricing and the price sensitivity of her customers were discussed. A variety of different advertising and promotional methods were also revealed. Finally, the group learned of a source of background information that might provide ideas and objectives not suggested by the conversation.

You should also note not only what was said in the conversation but also how it was said. Ms. Chelsea admitted that she had not kept up with her information gathering about her competition. Also, she was a bit unsure as to where Haggerty's should go next in their marketing strategy and planning. This is not to imply that Ms. Chelsea is not knowledgeable about her business. She has obviously demonstrated her ability to establish a loyal clientele and provide a good product. However, she would probably admit that there is very little about which she is certain. And, it is likely that she does not have a written marketing plan to follow. This will obviously impact her ability to make major marketing strategy decisions.

Ms. Chelsea's uncertainty about her customers and competitive environment offers an excellent opportunity for the group to provide her with valuable information. Even if nothing new, unique or surprising is revealed during the marketing planning process, the findings should serve to reduce her uncertainty and provide her with a basis for stronger confidence in what she believes. It is also quite possible that the marketing plan, when complete, will provide a valuable tool that can be revised annually. Sometimes, it is just a matter of writing a plan for the first time that breaks the barriers created by the overwhelming nature of this task. Both you and your client will be surprised at how easy it is to write a marketing plan when you follow the outline provided in this manual.

Appendix 3A contains a client interview form that you could use to guide you in asking key questions during the client interview. It is unlikely to include all of the important questions you will want to ask the client. However, it should encourage you to explore the major areas of marketing strategy and planning.

APPENDIX 3A
CLIENT INTERVIEW FORM

NAME OF FIRM _____

ADDRESS _____

CONTACT _____ PHONE_____

GENERAL INFORMATION:

Years in operation and background: _____

_____

_____

Major products, product lines, or services: _____

_____

_____

CUSTOMERS:

Geographical distribution: _____

Descriptive Characteristics (Age, Sex, Income, Occupation, Marital Status, etc.):_____

_____

_____

_____

Do you have customer groups that differ significantly from each other? If so, how? _____

_____

_____

Are there customer groups you think you should be reaching but aren't? If so, what do you think is the reason they aren't being reached?

_____

_____

_____

Are all of your potential customer groups sufficiently aware of your product or service? If yes, why do you think that? If not, why not?

_____

_____

COMPETITION:

Who do you believe to be your major competitor(s) and what is (are) the particular strength(s) of each?

COMPETITOR   **MAJOR STRENGTHS**

_____   _____

_____   _____

_____   _____

_____   _____

_____   _____

PRICING:

How important is pricing in maintaining your competitive position? _____

_____

How are your prices compared to your competitor(s)? _____

_____

How do you set your prices or make price changes? _____

_____

ADVERTISING:

How important is advertising in maintaining your competitive position? _____

_____

What does your advertising say?_____

_____

How much (or how often) do you advertise? _____

_____

Where do you advertise? _____

_____

Do your competitors advertise more or less than you do? _____

_____

Do you think their advertising is effective? _____

_____

SALES PROMOTION:

Are sales, special prices, coupons or other promotional items important to the success of your business?

_____

_____

Which kinds do you and your competitors use? _____

_____

_____

Do you use these methods to attract new customers or to build loyalty among existing customers?

_____

DISTRIBUTION OR LOCATION:

How important is distribution or location in maintaining your competitive position?

_____

How is your location compared to your competitors? _____

_____

PERSONAL SELLING AND CUSTOMER SERVICE:

How important is personal selling and/or customer service in maintaining your competitive position?

_____

How is your sales staff compared to your competitor(s)? _____

_____

MAJOR DECISIONS:

Are there major decisions in any area of your business that you are contemplating within the next year?

Decision #1: _____

Major alternatives: _____

Greatest uncertainty about alternatives: _____

What would you like to know that would help reduce this uncertainty? _____

_____

Decision #2: _____

Major alternatives: _____

Greatest uncertainty about alternatives: _____

What would you like to know that would help reduce this uncertainty? _____

_____

OTHER INFORMATION:

CHAPTER FOUR
PRESENTING INFORMATION

INTRODUCTION

When you provide a client with a business report, you are making a statement about your professional competence. A written report is a permanent record. You will want to create a product that is handsome, informative, and professional.

The purpose of this chapter is to guide you in preparing an outstanding report. Today, computer graphics and laser printers make it possible for anyone to create an appealing manuscript. Substance is not enough; you also need polish!

COMPETING INFORMATION

The information that you present to the client is competing with the information from many other sources. Most managers receive some sort of printout from their computer programs. At the very least, they receive information from their accountants, trade organizations, and state or local licensing agencies. Your report is in competition for the limited time of this manager. He/she is likely to devote more time to the information that is exciting, easy to read, and well-organized.

THE REPORT

Your report should be based on the outline that is presented in Chapter Five. If you follow this outline, you will have a well-organized document. The reader should understand the logical sequence of the report.

Besides the outline, there are some simple suggestions for a strong presentation. Here are some guidelines:

1. Include all of the information that you use to make your recommendations. Don't assume that the client knows everything about the product or service.

2. Use footnotes or end notes to cite your sources of information.

3. Create a filing system for all of the extra information that you acquire. Keep this on hand, and if the client has further questions, refer to the file for information.

4. Present all data in tables, charts, and graphs. Use a logical numbering system for this purpose.

5. If you plan a formal presentation of the document, either to the client or to your class, make overhead transparencies of the charts and tables.

6. Prepare the entry report on one word processor. Use a common system such as WordPerfect 5.1. Offer the disks to your client.

7. Use a laser quality printer for the report. Also, use the same printer for the entire document.

8. If you do not have a competent typist in your group, hire one. The same applies for creating graphs and charts.

9. Do not assign document preparation as a punishment. Many groups assign the typing to one person who has not been an active group member throughout the project. This person is supposed to make up for their lack of participation by preparing the document.

10. Take the final document to a print shop. Have it bound and make a title page.

These are some simple rules for document preparation. We do not mean to suggest, however, that a neat looking report will make up for poor execution of the project. Each report should contain substantive recommendations, based on proper and critical thinking. However, even the best information is lost if the style of the presentation is lacking.

WHAT THE CLIENT NEEDS TO KNOW

Your client needs to know two things. They are:

1.   Your recommendations or findings, and

2.   How you arrived at these decisions.

Your report, then, must contain all of the information necessary to meet the client's needs. If you follow the outline carefully, you will accomplish this. There are, however, some common mistakes that students make when they first prepare reports. Here are some:

1.   Be careful when making "all inclusive" statements. Try to avoid words such as "always or never" when referring to market situations. Marketing is dynamic and it is unlikely that "everyone would want to do anything always."

2.   Try to avoid inconsistency in using first, second, and third person pronouns. The third person is probably the best choice for a marketing plan document.

3.   Check your math. It is easy to make mistakes.

4.   Read the finished product out loud. Sometimes your ears will pick up mistakes that your eyes miss.

5.   Allow enough time for the project. This is a substantial task. Start your project early in the semester and finish early as well.

USING TABLES, GRAPHS, AND FIGURES

Appendix 4A contains some examples of graphs and charts. Notice that each graph contains an explanation directly beneath it. Do not assume that everyone will immediately understand the graph. Its impact often takes time. An explanation helps the reader to comprehend the full significance of the information.

Place tables into the text. Try not to use phrases such as "The Table below..." or "In the following Table..." The layout of the document may change. Then, the reader is left guessing as to which table is supposed to follow the statement.

Set up a numbering system for all tables, graphs, figures, and charts. You will notice that in this book, we differentiate between tables and figures. For example, in Chapter Six, Table 6.1, "Haggerty's Benefit/Segment Matrix" contains words and phrases. Conversely, Figure 6.1, "The Marketing Strategy Grid" contains a drawing.

SUMMARY

Spend some extra time organizing and printing your project. We cannot guarantee that it will result in a higher grade, but your client will love it. Also, you will be proud of the finished product.

Be imaginative and creative. After all, you are a marketer. Your style of presentation could be your competitive edge.

APPENDIX 4A
TYPICAL GRAPHS AND CHARTS

This Appendix contains examples of typical graphs and charts that will enhance your presentation.

From Table 6.4

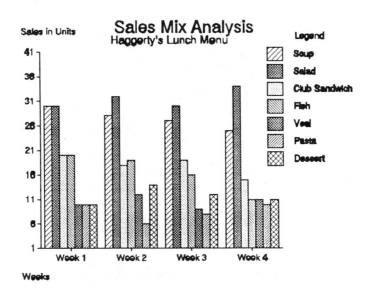

Bar Charts are excellent for comparing performance over time. This chart is taken, in part, from Table 6.4. It shows that the salad was the most frequently ordered item each week. In addition, it demonstrates that the number of salads ordered each week rose from 29 in week 1 to 33 in week 4.

A Bar Chart can be used to compare the performance of items against each other or against themselves. It is easy to read.

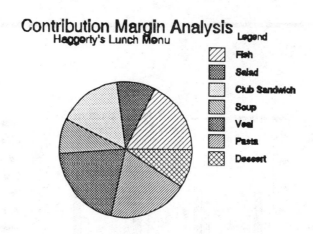

A Pie Chart provides a snapshot of a market or situation. It shows the relative percentage that each item represents. In this case, taken from Table 6.2, the pie chart shows the relative strength or weakness of each menu item's contribution margin.

Use pie charts when you want to illustrate relative position of each item.

From Table 6.2

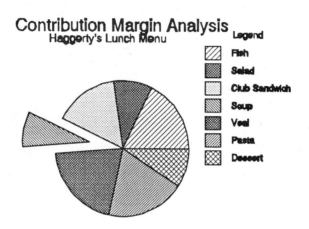

Contribution Margin Analysis
Haggerty's Lunch Menu

Legend
- Fish
- Salad
- Club Sandwich
- Soup
- Veal
- Pasta
- Dessert

An exploded pie chart emphasizes one portion of the pie. In this case, taken from Table 6.2, the relative weakness of the soup's contribution margin is shown.

Use an exploded pie chart when one item's strength or weakness will be better portrayed by a picture. It adds emphasis to the analysis.

CHAPTER FIVE
THE THREE-PART MARKETING PLAN

OUTLINE

Below is the complete outline for a three-part marketing plan. It is very detailed and somewhat lengthy. We tried to make it as complete as possible so that you would feel comfortable with it. You will find that the unique numbering system makes it easy to refer to various parts of the plan. The chapters of this manual are designed to help you complete the plan for your client.

This plan outline is taken from a graduate course that was offered at Florida International University by Mr. Dennis Marzella. Mr. Marzella is now a Vice President for Robinson, Yesawich, and Pepperdine, a marketing firm in Orlando.

THE THREE-PART SYSTEM

1.0 SITUATION ANALYSIS

      1.1   Your Company
               -- a one page description of your company
               -- the mission of your company
               -- who will be involved in the marketing effort

1.2   Your Product(s)/Service(s)
-- a list of each product
-- the benefits the product(s) offers the end-user
-- research that demonstrates the customers' perceptions of each product
-- the strengths of each product
-- the weaknesses of each product
-- if the product should be sold with others

1.3   The Price/Contribution Margin
-- prices of each product
-- contribution margin
-- competitors' prices
-- specials and discounts
-- sales mix calculations

1.4   Promotions
-- a list, with enclosures, of all promotions: advertising, public relations, sales, and
        publicity
-- the goal of each promotion
-- the effectiveness of each promotion: sales increases, customer feedback, etc.
-- the cost of each promotion compared to the revenue generated
-- the technical success or failure of each promotion

1.5   Sales
-- a list of salespeople
-- their quotas
-- the success rate of quotas
-- the profit/loss of the sales force when sales are compared to costs

1.6   Distribution
-- how the product is distributed
-- the distributors
-- product markup
-- channel integration
-- effectiveness of the distribution system

1.7   Competitive Analysis
-- a detailed list of the competition
-- products, prices
-- names and addresses of competition, their distributors, and their distributors'
        salespeople
-- market-share estimates of each competitor
-- strengths and weaknesses of each competing product

1.8   The Current Market
       -- a detailed description of the current market
       -- a list of market segments and their size
       -- frequency of use of each product in each segment
       -- level of demand in each segment
       -- recent trends that have affected the market
       -- your company's present position within each market segment (as perceived by the
              customer and in relation to the competition)
       -- your company's penetration in each segment
       -- a total picture of the market and your company's overall standing within it

1.9   Environmental Forces in the Market
       -- uncontrollable variables in your market
       -- economic factors
       -- legal variables
       -- political variables
       -- social variables in the market segments
       -- technological advances or changes

1.10   The Market Strategy Grid
       -- a graph that pictorially represents your position in the market, in relation to
              competitors and to market strength

1.11   Situation Analysis Summary

1.12   The Marketing Information System

2.0 MARKETING STRATEGIES

2.1   Major Strategy Statement
       -- a two- to three-sentence statement, describing the market position your company
              wants to obtain
       -- Relevance Statements (reasons supporting the Major Strategy Statement)

2.2   Objectives
       -- statements of goals, including new products, market share, rate of interest, etc.
       -- short- (6 months), mid- (6 months - 2 years), and long-term objectives (2 - 5
              years)

2.3   Basic Selling Idea (BSI)
-- statement of product benefits for the consumer
-- the consumers' viewpoint
-- Relevance Statements (reasons supporting the BSI)

2.4   The Market: Sources of Business
-- primary, secondary, and tertiary segments
-- size of each segment
-- expected growth
-- penetration factors
-- expected revenue (price x penetration)

2.5   Price Strategy
-- broad description of the price strategy
-- trends in competitors' prices
-- description of impending price changes

2.6   Promotion Strategy
-- broad description of the promotion strategy
-- trends in competitors' promotions
-- descriptions of impending promotional changes

2.7   Product Strategy
-- broad description of the product strategy
-- trends in competitors' strategies
-- description of new product developments

2.8   Distribution Strategy
-- broad description of the distribution strategy
-- trends in competitors' strategies
-- expected new directions for distribution

3.0   ACTION PLANS
-- date and number
-- title of the plan
-- person in charge
-- objectives
-- plan of action
-- time frame
-- cost
-- method of evaluation

3.1   Establishing the Marketing Budget

3.2   Evaluating the Action Plans

USING THE OUTLINE

You may be thinking, "Well, if all I have to do is fill in the outline, there will not be much room for creativity." This is certainly not the case. Marketing depends on creativity. Fortunately, with a plan, you only have to be creative ONE TIME. Once the plan is completed, creative energies can be directed towards customer satisfaction and making money.

Do not be afraid to follow the outline exactly. If you do, it will help you to produce a terrific document. Your client will find it easy to follow. Also, they can update it annually.

You may want to assign various parts of the Situation Analysis to members of your group. Complete each major section first, however, before going on to the next one. It is fine to split up the Situation Analysis, but it is very difficult to begin the Strategy until all the current information is available.

The next three chapters will lead you through the entire plan. Read the entire manual first before starting the plan. You will be proud of the finished product. Good luck with your first role as a marketing consultant.

CHAPTER SIX
THE SITUATION ANALYSIS

INTRODUCTION

In this chapter, you will actually begin the writing of your marketing plan. You will also see excerpts from Haggerty's marketing plan.

The Situation Analysis is the first step in developing your marketing system. It describes the competition, various consumer segments, and past and present market trends.

A needed product alone does not guarantee success. Especially if that product enters a marketplace where competition is fierce, demand is weak, and supply is strong. By predicting what you as a marketer and your product can expect, the Situation Analysis prepares you for problems which can prove devastating if not anticipated.

This chapter contains exercises to help you write your own Situation Analysis.

1.0   SITUATION ANALYSIS

Before you can decide on a direction, you must be sure of where you are. The Situation Analysis provides the fundamental information necessary to obtain a company's present position. In this section, we will examine all of the parts of the Situation Analysis. Exercises will be provided where necessary to assist you in completing the Situation Analysis for your organization.

1.1   Your Company.

Use this section to completely describe the organization that you are studying. Some managers might find this section to be a bit superfluous. However, it is always good to put the current organization into perspective. Sometimes, slight differences in company history can provide new perspectives for future marketing.

In this section, we will describe Haggerty's restaurant/bar. Haggerty's was built in 1987. It is a privately owned and operated facility. There are two main dining areas. They are referred to as the "Cork Room" and the "Eatery." The Eatery is the larger of the two rooms, seating approximately 150. The Cork Room seats 100. It has a separate entrance and can be used for private groups.

The bar area is referred to simply as "The Pub." It seats approximately 60 people. The pub is a popular spot for both drinking and dining.

Haggerty's serves a menu that features a mixture of traditional pub food and some new, trendy foods. The restaurant prides itself on excellent food and exceptional service. They feel that the only way to build a loyal clientele is to provide a consistent quality. The chef was hired from a small Inn in New England, where he had earned a strong reputation. However, the restaurant has always operated in a team concept. If the chef should leave, others have already been trained so that the consistency will remain.

Ms. Amanda Chelsea is the manager. She splits her time between the kitchen and the dining areas. The company policy is to have a manager who is always available to the guests. If something goes wrong, Ms. Chelsea's job is to correct it immediately. The restaurant has an interesting goal: "No customer should leave the premises dissatisfied." Ms. Chelsea realizes that in a service business, it is always possible for mistakes to occur. However, she, or the manager on duty, is authorized to provide complimentary meals or take something off the bill if a customer is not happy with it. If the service is bad, the customer will be invited back -- at the restaurant's expense.

Haggerty's Mission Statement

Haggerty's is a full service restaurant that serves only high quality food and drinks. We will do our best to create a loyal clientele.

Haggerty's is designed to create a family atmosphere and to serve the needs of both our guests and our employees. We offer our guests the highest standards in service and consistency. Our employees will receive fair treatment, stable jobs, and a profitable work environment.

Our goal is to be recognized as a dependable, permanent member of the hospitality community. To this end, we guarantee all of our products and services.

Your Client's Company Description

When you write Section 1.1 for your project, be sure to include all of the information that you can gather: address, phone number, organizational chart, etc. Also, if the organization does not have a mission statement, this is a good time to write one.

1.2   Your Product(s)/Service(s).

Most organizations have a variety of products/services that are offered to their customers. It is rare to find a company with a single product. Product and service packages combine different offerings for specific segments. In this section, you will describe, in detail, the various products that are available from your client.

There are two ways of looking at a product. The first perspective is that of the manufacturer. This is necessary for developing production standards and accounting practices. However, the more important way is from the viewpoint of the consumer. When you do your project, learn to look at products and services from the viewpoint of the ultimate customer.

At Haggerty's the chef sometimes wants to experiment with food. However, most guests do not want something that is totally unfamiliar. They are hesitant to spoil a meal by venturing too far into the unknown.

One of the most helpful tools for looking at products through the eyes of the customer is to perform a Benefit/Segment Matrix. In the following pages, you will learn how to develop this valuable tool.

The Benefit/Segment Matrix

Your product can probably be used in a variety of market segments. In fact, one marketing strategy is to develop new markets for your product by promoting new uses. This approach was used by Arm & Hammer for their baking soda.

Baking soda was originally designed as an ingredient for baking. With the advent of packaged mixes, this use declined since people less frequently baked from scratch. Changing demographics such as the increase in working mothers have created new markets for the cake and cookie mix industry. Now, baking soda is promoted as a refrigerator and carpet deodorizer, as well as a substitute for toothpaste. These are certainly varied uses for the same product.

Haggerty's has a variety of products and a number of market segments. They could actually construct a very large Benefit/Segment Matrix. Some of the products/services that they offer are: lunch, dinner, happy hour, meeting facilities, private group catering, late night dinner, early bird specials, post-game parties, etc.

Each of these product packages has a unique appeal to the various market segments that Haggerty's serves. Below is a small Matrix for some of the products.

TABLE 6.1
HAGGERTY'S BENEFIT/SEGMENT MATRIX

Product/Service

Segment	Lunch	Dinner	Early Bird	Catering
Local Business People	S	M	L	S
Singles	L	S	L	L
Seniors	L	M	S	L
University Students	L	S	M	L
Couples	M	S	M	L
Families	L	M	S	L

S = STRONG   M = MEDIUM   L = LIGHT

While a full Matrix would be larger, this example does provide the essence of the information that is necessary. Notice that Seniors have a strong demand for the early bird special. Families do as well. However, couples, who perhaps want to get away from the family, are more likely to have a later dinner.

The Benefit/Segment Matrix can provide some useful information in examining the product offering through the eyes of the customer. It forces the planner to identify all of the products and to begin the segmentation process.

A Matrix helps identify market opportunities. The grid should be current. When a new use or benefit for the product is discovered, the marketer incorporates it into the grid and introduces the new benefit to current customers, while locating new market segments.

Appendix 6A contains an exercise for completing a Benefit/Segment Matrix for this project.

1.3   The Price/Contribution Margin.

Many marketers feel that price analysis merely means listing the wholesale or retail price of a product. This is only part of the formula. Selling price is important. It represents the profit potential of an organization. Set too high, it may discourage customers. Set too low, it could mean the death of an organization.

More important than the price of a product is the contribution margin that it produces. A discussion of contribution margin is found in Chapter 9. Basically, the contribution margin is that portion of the selling price that remains after subtracting the variable costs. The contribution margin is used to offset the fixed costs. When all of the fixed costs are covered, the contribution margin turns into profit.

In this section of the project, you should list all of the prices for all of the goods and services that are offered by your client. This can be a daunting task. It is one of the reasons that we suggest that you use a small business rather than a large conglomerate.

Let's examine some of the prices and contribution margins for Haggerty's restaurant. The system that we will use, while applied specifically to a restaurant, can be used for any type of business.

TABLE 6.2
THE LUNCH MENU AT HAGGERTY'S

Item	Cost	Selling Price	Contribution Margin
Soup	$ .30	$2.50	$2.20
Salad	.45	3.00	2.55
Club Sandwich	.80	5.00	4.20
Fish	2.20	6.95	4.75
Veal	2.00	7.50	5.50
Pasta	.80	5.90	5.10
Dessert	.50	3.00	2.50

Some interesting facts surface when analyzing the menu in Table 6.2. Notice that the contribution from the pasta dish is higher than the contribution from the fish dish. The pasta dish sells for $1.05 less than the fish dish. Yet, each time someone orders pasta instead of fish, the restaurant makes an additional $.35 in contribution margin. Which dish would you rather sell?

The Price and the Sales Mix

The sales mix is the ratio of products that are sold. For example, if a company has two products, A and B, the sales mix could have several possibilities. Examine the two sales mixes in Table 6.3. They provide some valuable insight.

TABLE 6.3
TWO SAMPLE SALES MIXES

Sales Mix 1

	Sales Price	Contribution Margin	Number Sold	Total Contribution
Product A	$50	$30	40	$1,200
Product B	$60	$25	60	$1,500
TOTAL			100	$2,700

Sales Mix 2

	Sales Price	Contribution Margin	Number Sold	Total Contribution
Product A	$50	$30	60	$1,800
Product B	$60	$25	40	$1,000
TOTAL			100	$2,800

Notice that, in both sales mix 1 and sales mix 2, 100 units were sold. However, in sales mix 2, the contribution margin was $100 higher. The sales mix has a very definite effect on the contribution margin.

You can increase the profitability of your client's organization by designing a plan that changes the sales mix. A sales mix that produces a higher average contribution margin will produce greater profits while serving the same number of customers. The results of the sales mix/contribution margin calculations are called the Weighted Average Contribution Margin.

In Table 6.4, two sales mixes are shown for Haggerty's. Sales mix 1 represents the situation BEFORE a training program was instituted for the waiters. In sales mix 2, the waiters have been trained to sell more pasta dishes. Also, they were urged to sell more salads to accompany the meals. For the same number of customers at lunch, Haggerty's is now making more money.

TABLE 6.4
TWO SALES MIXES FOR HAGGERTY'S

Sales Mix 1

Item	# Sold	Unit Contribution Margin	Total Contribution Margin
Soup	30	$2.20	$ 66.00
Salad	30	2.55	76.50
Club Sandwich	20	4.20	84.00
Fish	20	4.75	95.00
Veal	10	5.50	55.00
Pasta	10	5.10	51.00
Dessert	10	2.50	25.00
TOTAL			$452.50

Sales Mix 2

Item	# Sold	Unit Contribution Margin	Total Contribution Margin
Soup	30	$2.20	$ 66.00
Salad	40	2.55	102.00
Club Sandwich	20	4.20	84.00
Fish	10	4.75	47.50
Veal	10	5.50	55.00
Pasta	20	5.10	102.00
Dessert	10	2.50	25.00
TOTAL			$481.50

In both sales mixes, 60 entrees were sold. (To get this figure, add the number of people who purchased the entree items.) Yet, sales mix 2 produces $29 more in contribution margin. There are only two differences between the sales mixes.

In sales mix 2, the waiters managed to steer 10 of the guests from fish to pasta. Also, in sales mix 2, 10 more people purchased a salad to accompany their meal. The results: without increasing the number of customers, the company can increase profits by selling the products that make it the most money and by packaging products in bundles. This lesson is universal.

The increase in profits can only be attained, however, when the marketer clearly understands the consequences of price and costs. For a small company, this should be relatively easy to surmise.

Discounts

At this point, you should also examine the effects of discounting on the bottom line. In many cases, discounts will decrease the contribution margin. This happens every time a discount is not accompanied by a reduction in variable costs.

For example, at Haggerty's the early bird dinner is approximately 20% less than the usual menu. One of the most popular items is the Chicken Haggerty. It normally sells for $10 and costs $3 to produce. During the early bird special, it sells for $8. It still costs $3 to produce. Table 6.5 shows these calculations.

TABLE 6.5
DISCOUNTING PRICES

Regular Menu

Item	Selling Price	Cost	Contribution Margin
Chicken Haggerty	$10.00	$3.00	$7.00

Early Bird

Item	Selling Price	Cost	Contribution Margin
Chicken Haggerty	$8.00	$3.00	$5.00

The early bird menu, with its special prices, is called a sales promotion. It is a great idea -- in concept. Ms. Chelsea reasoned that the restaurant was already open during this normally slow period. The chefs, waiters, and other staff were in place. The fixed costs were also piling up. Yet, from 5:00 p.m. until 7:00 p.m., the dining rooms were relatively empty. So, she ran the early bird special to attract customers during this time.

There is only one catch. If the customers who come to the early bird are the same customers who would have come later, then she has not made more money. In fact, she has lowered the contribution margin by $3 per person.

YOU CAN USE PRICE/CONTRIBUTION MARGIN TO DETERMINE THE FINANCIAL FEASIBILITY OF MOST SALES PROMOTIONS. REMEMBER, INCREASING BUSINESS IS NOT THE KEY TO SUCCESS; INCREASING CONTRIBUTION MARGIN IS THE KEY.

Appendix 6B contains an exercise that will help you determine the contribution margin and sales mixes for your client.

1.4   Promotions.

Many managers equate promotions with marketing. Actually, as you know, promotion is only one of the four marketing mix variables. However, it has a tremendous importance in delivering the message to the customer.

In this section, you will analyze three categories of the current promotional efforts being made by the company. These will include advertising, publicity, and sales promotion. Personal selling, the fourth part of promotion, is considered separately.

Advertising

Ask your client for copies of all current and past advertising pieces. This would include brochures as well as newspaper, magazine, and broadcast media. Every bit of advertising material should already be assembled in a file. If it is not, you can perform a valuable service to the client by compiling all of this information.

Publicity

Your client has probably used some form of publicity in the past. Perhaps they were mentioned in a trade publication. They might have written some press releases. Whatever the form, assemble samples of this publicity and public relations for your files.

Sales Promotions

These would include contests, special events, coupons, trade shows, volume discounts, etc. Actually, sales promotion is often overlooked. Many companies tend to categorize their sales promotions as publicity. For example, publicity in the form of new releases can be used to increase attendance at sales promotion events.

Measuring Promotional Success

Once you have assembled all of the promotional materials, it is time to evaluate their success or failure. Actually, this should be done on an ongoing basis. However, particularly for a small business, it is likely that the manager has not made the complete analysis of promotions.

Each promotional campaign should have a goal. It may not be written or even clearly thought out. However, without a goal, you cannot measure the effectiveness of the promotion. If the manager is unable to furnish you with a goal for each promotion, you will have to create one. If there are no goals, it is likely that some money was wasted on promotions.

Appendix 6C contains an exercise for evaluating the effectiveness of promotions. Use the Price/Contribution Margin calculations and the information found in Chapter 9 to determine the financial success of each promotion (if applicable).

An Example of Promotional Analysis

Haggerty's has an early bird special menu that is designed to utilize the facilities in the off hours. They have used the following analysis for this sales promotion.

Haggerty's discounts its menu prices by about 20% for the two hour early bird special. They have three menu items on this special. The two sales mixes are contained in Table 6.6.

TABLE 6.6
A SALES PROMOTION

Regular Menu

Item	Price	Cost	Margin	Units Sold	Total Contribution
Chicken	$10	$3	$ 7	20	$140
Steak	15	5	10	10	100
Pasta	8	1	7	20	140
TOTAL				50	$380

Early Bird Menu

Item	Price	Cost	Margin	Sold	Contribution
Chicken	$ 8	$3	$5	20	$100
Steak	12	5	7	10	70
Pasta	6	1	5	20	100
TOTAL				50	$270

Notice that the proportion of the items sold is the same for each menu. Yet, the contribution is much less for the early bird special. The price is lower, but the costs are the same.

On a per person basis, the contribution margin for the regular menu is $7.60 ($380 divided by 50 people). The per person contribution margin for the early bird special is $5.40. This is a difference of $2.20 per person. We will use these figures to analyze the cost of the promotion for the early bird special.

Ms. Chelsea reports that she runs two advertisements per week in the local paper to promote the special. They cost $300 each. In addition, she runs two radio spots per day, four days per week. These spots cost $200 each. Her total weekly promotional costs are:

2 newspaper ads x $300	=	$ 600
2 radio spots per day @ $200 each x 4 days	=	$1600
Total	=	$2200

Haggerty's serves about 100 people per night, seven days per week, at the early bird special. Ms. Chelsea estimates that 10% of those people would have eaten at the normal time. But, they chose to go to the early bird to save money. This costs the restaurant contribution margin. Ms. Chelsea calculates that cost as follows:

100 people per day x 10% = 10 people
10 people x $2.20 (diff. in contrib. margin) = $22 per day
$22 x 7 days = $154

When added to the $2200 in promotional costs, this is $2354 per week to run the early bird.

The revenue is calculated as follows:

100 people per day x $5.40 contribution per person = $540 total
$540 daily x 7 days = $3,780 per week

Total Revenue	=	$3780
Total Expenses	=	$2354
New Contribution	=	$1426

So, the early bird special is a success. It produces $1,426 per week in unencumbered contributions. This is a total of $74,152 per year. It is enough to pay for Ms. Chelsea's salary plus benefits.

This is the type of analysis you should do for all of the major promotions. Obviously, you will not be able to do this for every promotion. Some will not generate revenues. Others are too small to bother with. However, you should find some way to evaluate each promotional activity.

In Appendix 6C, you will be asked to list each promotion and rate its success. If you have calculations to back up your evaluations, attach them to the form.

1.5   Sales.

Even though personal selling is only one form of promotion, it has such importance for most businesses that we suggest it be examined separately. In this section, you will compare the income generated by the sales force with the expenses that they incur. These would include salaries, commissions, meals, etc.

Most organizations use some kind of sales force. Some, at the very least, must take orders from the customers. In a service business, the sales force may also be the providers of the service. This is the case at Haggerty's. The waiters and waitresses are both the sales staff and the service providers.

The effectiveness of the sales staff can be measured in the same way as other promotions. We compare the cost of the staff to the contribution margin. If we run an incentive trip, the cost of the trip is compared to the extra value of the contribution that is generated. Let's look at an example of this.

A company sells office equipment for $1,000 per unit. The variable costs for each unit, including sales commissions, are $500. This yields a $500 contribution margin.

Jim, a sales rep, has a quota of 100 units this year. However, he is told that he will have the opportunity, after he reaches the quota, to open a new territory. If he sells 20 machines in the new territory, he will receive an incentive trip to Hawaii for 2. The cost of the trip to the company is $4,000.

Jim reaches his quota in October and begins work in the new territory. He has a number of expenses. They are listed below:

Airfare	$1,000
Hotel	500
Meals	500
Entertainment	1,000
Car Rental	500
Other	500
Total	$4,000
Incentive Trip	$4,000
Grand Total	$8,000

Jim sold the 20 units in the new territory. The company received $10,000 in contribution margin. Even after paying for the incentive trip and the other expenses, they retained $2,000 in contribution. In addition, they receive lasting benefits from opening a new territory.

Carefully calculate the effectiveness of the sales force for your client. Look for additional opportunities. Would increased commissions or wider territories improve individual performances? Make sure that the results of your analysis are based on contribution margin.

1.6   Distribution.

Marketers study distribution in order to facilitate the movement of goods and services. They want to put their products into the hands of the user. Speed of delivery, consistency and maintenance are all parts of distribution. The paths that products take, from manufacturer to wholesaler to retailer to consumer, are known as the Channels of Distribution.

Channel maintenance and management are an important part of marketing. In this section of the plan, you will analyze the effectiveness of the channels. Sometimes, a product misses a very valuable market segment because it is not in the correct channel.

Perrier water from France is an excellent example. It was originally distributed in liquor stores. Later, when it was distributed through convenience stores and supermarkets, it reached a much wider audience. It became an alternative to soft drinks.

Place

Marketers used to talk of the four P's of marketing: Product, Price, Promotion, and Place. In many cases, Place has now become distribution. For some companies, however, Place is still a marketing mix variable.

Haggerty's still uses Place analysis. The management is concerned with traffic, appearances, accessibility, and maintenance. Most service companies have a strong concern for Place. Retailers are also conscious of the effects of Place on image and performance. If customers visit the offices or property of your organization, use Place analysis to look at the physical plant from the viewpoint of the customer.

1.7   Competitive Analysis.

It is important to analyze the strengths and weaknesses of your competition. In a market where supply exceeds demand, competitors will go to great lengths to steal your business. You must be prepared to deal with them in the marketplace.

To "win" you must know as much as possible about your competitors and your competitors' product(s). This does not mean you must resort to illegal measures, but within the norms of competent business action, there are many ways to compile useful information that will help you get ahead.

The Best Source of Information

The best source of competitive information is from the competition. Purchase the products and visit the premises. Talk to their customers and read the trade journals as well.

One of the authors of this text was a consultant for a small hotel chain in New England. He visited the competition, stayed in their rooms, ate in their restaurants and talked to the employees. At night, he drove around the parking lots, looking at the license plates of the cars, determining the states of origin of the guests. He even counted the number of rooms that had lights on in the evening. This is an excellent indication of the occupancy percentage.

No matter what type of product or service your client represents, there is always some sort of competition. And, there are always imaginative, LEGAL, and ETHICAL ways to obtain competitive information.

We are continually amazed at how easy it is to collect competitive information. The products and employees of the competition can generally tell you all that you need to know. It is a good idea therefore, to warn employees about supplying too much information to an over-inquisitive stranger. The stranger could be the competition. Salespeople should be informative and courteous, and know when to refer certain individuals to management.

Haggerty's Competitive Information

Ms. Chelsea maintains rigorous records on her competition. She sends employees to the other restaurants to gather information. They note the number of people in the dining room, eating lines, menu items and prices, and daily specials. All of these are recorded on a personal computer.

She also reads the restaurant trade journals and the business section of the local paper. There is often advance news of new restaurant openings and managerial changes. She often knows more about a competitor's menu from last year than the current manager does.

Appendix 6D contains an exercise that will help you coordinate competitive information. You will probably have to adapt the form to fit the special needs of your client.

1.8   The Current Market.

In this section, you will analyze the depth of the current market, the size of each segment, and your client's relative position within each segment. If this sounds like a daunting task, refer to the section "Estimating the Size of the Market" in Chapter 9.

This part of the Situation Analysis is important for two reasons.

1.   It is essential to understand the workings of the marketplace, the make-up of the segments, and their importance to the businesses operating in that market.

2.   The ability to predict market trends and growth is the epitome of professional competence for a marketer. It is important that the people or person who develops the marketing plan should also be a master of segment analysis.

The first step in determining the market potential is to break the market into segments. The following section provides an exercise that will help you to do this.

Segmenting the Market

Why do liquor stores sell more beer and wine than scotch whiskey?
Why do some men color their hair while others let the gray show?
Why do some people bake from scratch, but others use a mix?

There are no simple answers to these questions; however, there is an underlying rationale for the differences in behavior among these groups. Let's look at the reasons why people use different products.

A Segmenting Example. When Lite Beer was first introduced, it was not sold by Miller. In fact, it was intended to be a low calorie beer for women who were conscious of their figures. The product was not a success, because the developer did not analyze the depth of the market segment that was targeted. Even if women did drink the new diet beer, how much would they drink? The next time you are in class, ask your instructor to conduct an experiment. Ask all of the women in class who drink more than a six pack of beer a day to raise their hands. Without getting into the moral implications of drinking too much beer, it is safe to say that the number of women responding affirmatively will be small. Actually, the number of men who admit to this behavior is also small. However, the seller of beer is looking for a consumer who drinks lots of beer. It's that simple.

The first variables to use when segmenting are the demographics. These include the following:

- age
- sex
- marital status
- renter or owner
- income
- family-size

These are easy to determine. The U.S. Census and other factual publications contain such data for many areas. But how are they useful in defining a market segment? They help us identify homogenous groups of people.

When Miller decided to enter the light beer market, they identified their primary segment: blue collar, 30 to 50 years old, married, moderate income, high school graduate. (We're just guessing here.) They specifically targeted their promotions for this group and have revolutionized the beer industry.

The purpose of using demographics is to create a picture of the "average" consumer most likely to buy your product. This doesn't mean there is only one kind of consumer. By lumping together the most common characteristics of the people who most often buy your product, you can know them better, and thus meet their needs more efficiently.

Heavy Users

It is usually wasteful to attempt to appeal to all consumers. Not everyone can or will buy a Volkswagen ... or a Cadillac. These automobiles are designed to meet the needs of different segments. Zeroing in on your primary-user segment(s) allows you to reach the greatest number of people interested in your product at a minimum of cost and time.

When Miller Lite introduced its beer, they looked for the segment that would drink low-calorie/low-alcohol beer the most. They could have focused in on diet-conscious women, promoting the low-calorie benefit of the beer, but demographics suggested that most women watching their weight avoid beer altogether. Instead, they focused in on men with common demographic features. They developed a slogan specifically for this individual: "Lite is less filling, so you can drink more." This is smart segmenting.

Miller used demographics to segment their market and researched usage-rate. Usage-rate is important. It is better to create a loyal clientele that frequently uses your product over one that doesn't. A car dealer wants customers to return each year to buy a new car. A toothpaste compan· wants its consumers to brush after every meal. Usage-rate is a tool for segmenting the market.

Haggerty's Usage Rate. Ms. Chelsea does not want to waste time promoting to people who only dine out once or twice a year. For example, Mother's Day and Valentine's Day are very busy in restaurants. However, Haggerty's will always be full on those days, no matter what promotions take place.

So, Ms. Chelsea wants to develop loyal customers from the "Dining Out" segment. She is interested in identifying people who eat at restaurants about twice a week. This is her heavy user segment.

Industrial Segments

So far we have only discussed end-users or consumers. There are also industrial segments that use products to make other products. There are several classifications of industrial products and users, but they share commonalities. In segmenting these markets, some of the same variables are used.

Industrial customers are segmented by the size of the company, the organization of the buying function, or the usage-rate of the product. Here again the concept of usage-rate is important. Sales calls are expensive. It is better to make a sales call that produces a large order rather than a small order.

Geography

Both consumer and industrial markets are segmented through the variable of geographic origin. The Louisiana World's Fair planners used geographic segmentation. They drew three circles around New Orleans on a map. The first circle had a radius of 50 miles. The second circle had a radius of 100, and the third circle, 150. The planners reasoned that the people living closest to the site of the fair were likely to visit it more often over the season than those living farther away. On the other hand, those living farther were more likely to visit the fair on more consecutive days.

The same segmentation technique is used in industry. Since a lumber wholesaler sells more lumber to customers in the northern states during summer than winter, the wholesaler adjusts promotions and pricing accordingly.

mary, Secondary, and Tertiary Segments

ever segmentation variables you use, some customer segments are more desirable than others. gments are larger, more affordable, less competitive or have some feature that makes them ealing. This is the primary segment.

ers prefer to identify at least three segments for targeting, primary through tertiary. a mix-and-serve snack cake example. The marketer may decide to target young mothers as the primary segment; they use the product most often. Grandmothers, the second largest user, make up the secondary segment, with adults who like snack cakes comprising the tertiary. The actual segmentation process is detailed and thorough, supported by observation, documentation, and research.

Haggerty's has two primary segments. They are 1) Local Business People (lunch and dinner meetings) and 2) Couples (who live in the area and leave the kids at home).

The Business People are drawn from the local office park and the many health care offices in the area. The usually have lunch out five times per week. Also, they schedule a number of dinner meetings in the Cork Room and use Haggerty's for office party catering. It is a strong, dependable segment.

The Couples market is drawn from the 25,000 homeowners who live within 6 square miles of the restaurant. They are all within a 15 minute drive. This is important, because research has shown that this group often goes out on the spur of the moment. They are not likely to travel farther for dinner.

Haggerty's has several other market segments. Ms. Chelsea states that Singles, including the students of a local University, are a strong secondary market segment. The Senior market is also relatively strong. In fact, the early bird segment is almost 60% seniors. Although Ms. Chelsea values each of these secondary segments, she does not plan events or initiate promotions that would bring the two groups to the restaurant at the same time. Unfortunately, happy hour and the early bird special are roughly the same time. This has been a problem in the past, because neither group feels comfortable with the other. For this reason, the Pub is kept separate from the dining room.

A Necessary Step - Analysis of Market Segments

A thorough analysis of the market segments is imperative. Without it, the marketing plan cannot be written. Each segment will have a marketing mix that is specifically developed to fit the needs of those customers. For example, Haggerty's managers would adjust their marketing mix variables as follows:

Local Business People

Product   - a guaranteed "Quick Lunch" that gets workers back to the office

Price   - a range of prices that are suitable for personal dining and that fall within expense account limits

Promotion	- advertisements in the business section of the paper, drive time radio spots
Place	- good parking facilities and visibility to office park

Senior Market

Product	- an early bird special menu with quick service and good portions
Price	- special discounts for Senior Citizens and the early bird prices
Promotions	- coupons and advertisements in the newspaper and on Senior-oriented radio programs
Place	- easy accessibility, ramps, and bright lights at tables

From the above, it should be apparent that without segmenting the market, it is difficult to develop marketing mix variables that will be meaningful in attracting the various types of guests.

Appendix 6E contains an exercise that will help you to analyze the market segments for your client.

Predicting Market Growth or Decline

Once you have identified the segments that are operating in your market, selected possible targets, and defined their constituencies, it is possible to build a meaningful picture of the market as a whole.

There are many sources available to marketers for prediction information. The important thing to remember is that you will never be completely sure of your prediction. By this, we mean that no one can predict the future. You are trying to put together enough information to make a reasonable guess.

Types Of Data

There are two basic types of data: primary and secondary. Primary data is gathered specifically for your client. You may do it or someone else may. Secondary data was gathered for general use, usually by a government or trade association. It is not as useful, but it costs less. Use both types.

To gather market information:

1.   Stay abreast of industry trends

2.   Examine secondary data from your market area

3.   Use primary data from your client

It is interesting to note that we suggest that you get primary data from your client. The business records probably contain a wealth of information. If they do not, or if your client is not willing to share this information, observe the customers yourself. Make notes on your client as you would on a competitor.

An Example

Ms. Chelsea is eager to determine if her segments are growing or declining. Her first concern is for the Local Business People. You take the following steps.

1.   Visit the local Chamber of Commerce to determine the relative growth or decline of businesses in the area.

2.   Drive around the area. Stay within ten minutes of the restaurant. Ms. Chelsea says that this is about the farthest a regular lunch customer will drive.

3.   Look for new office construction.

4.   Call the managers of the local office parks and industrial centers to ask how many people work in the parks.

5.   Make a reasonable guess as to how many business people are in the ten minute area.

6.   Call a local commercial real estate agency and ask for their predictions as to growth or decline in this area.

7.   Make a final estimate of the percentage increase or decrease in this segment.

You are probably thinking "That's not too specific. What if I'm wrong?" You probably will not be EXACTLY right. But, you have to make a guess. Your informed estimate will be as reliable as the time and information that you put into it.

Appendix 6F contains an exercise to help you put together some market growth or decline information.

1.9   Environmental Forces in the Market.

All companies operate within an environment that presents the marketer with challenges beyond his or her control. These challenges are created by the environmental variables.

While the environment is beyond the control of the marketers, they must still work within the dynamic constraints of the business and political arenas. The marketer exercises control over the marketing mix variables to achieve the goals of the operation within these dynamics. By altering product, price, promotion, and distribution, marketers create adaptable strategies.

There are five environmental variables: legal, social, technological, economic and political. Sometimes, these variables affect the industry as a whole, while others present regional and local challenges. In this section, we will examine the possible ramifications of these uncontrollable variables on the marketing analysis of Haggerty's as an illustration of marketing mix adjustment in a changing environment.

Legal and Political

The dynamic nature of the federal, state, and local political and legal environments has certainly affected the marketing of the restaurant. Perhaps the most outstanding change, in recent years, has been the legislation regarding third party liability for alcohol abuse.

Under third party liability, a restaurant or bar can be held liable for damages caused by one of its patrons. So, if a bartender serves alcohol to a guest who is already drunk and that guest then gets in an automobile and injures someone else, the injured party can recover damages from the restaurant. How has this affected the marketing mix variables?

Product. During the first year of operation, Haggerty's had a very popular happy hour. It lasted from 5:00 p.m. until 7:00 p.m. During the first hour, patrons paid $5. They then received all the drinks they could hold. In the second hour, it was a two for one special. There was very little food served. This practice exposed Haggerty's to liability. Also, it put their guests in danger.

Now, prices are reduced on some drinks during happy hour. However, the Pub features a wide variety of snack foods. In fact, the small buffet includes a carved roast beef. The emphasis is no longer on consuming as much alcohol as possible.

This change has been well received. True, some of the original happy hour crowd has moved on. These were younger, less affluent customers. They have been replaced by a more suitable clientele. The new group is also more likely to stay for dinner.

Price. Haggerty's offers free soda and coffee in the Pub. This allows the designated driver to spend an evening for free.

Promotion. Haggerty's has been featured in several regional newspapers for its approach to drinking. The articles are the result of some press releases that were made by Ms. Chelsea.

Place. There were no changes in Place due to this environmental variable. However, Haggerty's will renovate some of their facilities to meet the needs of the Americans With Disabilities Act - another legal change.

Technological

The major effects of technological change have been in the Product area. Microwave cooking has increased the speed of food preparation. It can cause problems though. Guests are sometimes put off by food that they know is microwaved. Haggerty's has hired Chef-Instructors from the local culinary school to demonstrate innovative uses for the microwave.

Social

Some of the recent changes in social behavior have given Haggerty's some terrific opportunities. The most important change has been the number of women in the workplace.

The "Modern Woman" no longer has to stay at home all day, cooking, cleaning, and taking care of the children. Now, she can work eight hours, then come home and take care of the children, cook, and clean. What an improvement!

The change in work habits has brought two changes in buying behavior. First, because of disposable income, the new family dines out more often. This is obviously good for a restaurant. Second, the family is likely to MEET at the restaurant. One of the parents picks the kids up from the babysitter and meets the other parent at the restaurant.

This second change has affected Haggerty's. They now need a larger parking lot to accommodate the cars. The early bird special is designed, in part, to compete for these family guests. A children's menu has been added. A separate entrance to the dining room was added to allow families to enter the restaurant without passing through the Pub. Finally, advertisements have been run showing a smiling waitress serving some children. Many families are afraid that they will not be welcome with children. Haggerty's wants them to know that this is not a problem.

It could be a problem for other guests, however. To alleviate this, the families are all seated in the Cork Room. This adjustment to Place helps keep the families away from other guests.

Economic

The recession has cost Haggerty's some business. Job losses in the defense industry have closed one of the leading employers in the area. This hurt the restaurant at lunch. To combat this, Haggerty's has not increased prices and, in some cases, created new menu items that are low cost yet high contribution margin specials.

The changes have worked out well. Pasta dishes are now very popular. As we have seen earlier in this book, this can mean a better return on the bottom line -- and savings for the guest. This is a great combination.

Summary

The environmental variables are uncontrollable. Yet, they may present opportunities for the smart marketer. Although most people do not want to deal with change, it can be very healthy. A company's ability to foresee and act upon environmental changes could provide a competitive advantage.

The exercise in Appendix 6G will help you to scan the environment for your client.

1.10   The Market Strategy Grid.

A marketer can only appreciate this section of the Situation Analysis after it has been completed. Without this positioning tool, it is difficult to develop manageable strategies. Read this section completely first, then place your client's company on the grid.

Grid Development

There are a number of ways to visually display your position in relation to the competition. The Market Strategy Grid (MSG)[1] is one of the best ways and should be completed at the end of the Situation Analysis, before the strategy section. It provides a reference point for the development of competitive strategies. From the grid, you can visualize the strategy techniques necessary to successfully position your product and compete.

---

[1]Nykiel, Ronald K. "Marketing In The Hospitality Industry," 2nd Edition, 1984, Von Noutrand, pp. 55-64.

It is easy to locate your product and your competitors' products when they are displayed on a grid. Examine the grid format in Figure 6.1, read the explanations for each position on the grid, and begin thinking like a market strategist.

FIGURE 6.1
THE MARKETING STRATEGY GRID

		MARKET DEMAND		
		Strong	Moderate	Weak
B E	Full	1 a	2	3
N E F	Medium	b 4 c	5	6
I T S	Limited	d 7 e	8	9

The horizontal axis represents the strength or potential strength of market demand. The vertical axis represents the amount of benefits offered by each product, with the most benefits at the top and the least at the bottom. A position on the right side of the grid represents weak market demand; on the left, strong market demand. After careful consideration of the market and its potential growth or decline, you can place your product on the horizontal axis.

A product located in box 2, for example, has a full range of benefits (vertical axis) and expects a moderate market demand (horizontal axis). Your product's position on the vertical axis is determined by evaluating the number of benefits it offers in relation to the benefits that could be offered. Use the Benefit/Segment Matrix you completed in Appendix 6A to position your company, then use the same type of analysis to position your competitors.

Haggerty's Position on the Grid

There are 5 companies located on the grid in Figure 6.1. They are located by the letters a, b, c, d, and e. Haggerty's is letter c. It is in the middle part of box 2. This means that the market demand is strong, but the number and types of services that Haggerty's offers are somewhat limited. Restaurant b is still within box 2, but it has a larger menu, more banquet rooms, and a lower guest to waiter ratio. They need more waiters, because the menu is more complicated.

There is also a restaurant in box 1. This restaurant is a full service, French cuisine establishment. Notice that the demand for this type of restaurant is slightly less. However, there really is no competition for them. Their prices are high, so volume can be low.

In box 7, there are two restaurants. These are limited menu and quick service. They charge less per person and hope to make up the difference through volume. However, they also have a smaller payroll and less inventory to worry about.

In this case, all of these restaurants are making money and are well positioned for the clientele that they serve.

Placing Your Company on the Grid

Appendix 6H contains an exercise for putting your company, and its competitors, on the grid. Once you have accomplished this, you should begin to formulate some strategies. The outline below will assist you in setting some realistic strategies for your positioned company.

Market Strategies

Box 1 - In this position, you will want to raise prices to the maximum that the market will bear. Demand is strong. You will have a full range of benefits to offer.

Heighten the image of luxury through careful promotion. Volume is not as important as price and quality. Maintain the premises, hire very well-trained staff. Offer the best service possible. Your strategy should be to maintain this position.

Box 2 - While this is still a great position, it is not as advantageous as 1. Undertake a marketing strategy that will solidify your image. Use promotion to increase demand for the market as a whole, and your product in particular. Keep prices high but be willing to package the product with other high quality offerings.

Box 3 - This is a dangerous position. You have a high priced, high cost product in a weak demand. Concentrate on the market. Find new sources of business. Offer a discounted version of the product with fewer benefits.

Box 4 - This is a very advantageous position. Concentrate on service and quality with the limited benefits. Do less than products in 1, but do it well. Try to raise prices to the threshold of difference between 1 and 4.

Box 5 - Concentrate on alternative market sources. Keep quality high but do not increase the number of benefits too much. If the market slips, you will then be in position 6. Promote the alternative uses for the product.

Box 6 - Look for market opportunities and use price to attract new sources. But, do not lower price unless the volume will make up for it. Consider a massive overhaul of distribution. Get the product into more distributorships. Perhaps identify alternative sales forces that have lower costs and greater market potential.

Box 7 - Maintain the limited service offerings. Control all costs so that price can remain low. However, raise prices to the threshold of difference between your product and those in 4. Serve the masses through a dedication to promotion and distribution. Do not make it difficult for people to get your product.

Box 8 - You are in a medium market, but dependent on volume. Concentrate on increasing demand. If necessary, increase the number of benefits to move into box 5. From there, you can demand a higher price.

Box 9 - Consider alternative uses for the product. Perhaps it is time to sell out and retire. When demand is low and benefits are limited, it will not be long before the product is defunct. If the product is part of a very wide line, keep it around. It may help to sell other models or products. If the company only has one product, tear down the buildings, and be happy that you at least still have your health.

Actually, we do not want to be cynical, but it is important for young marketers to realize that not all problems can be solved. Products in boxes 3, 6 and 9 are in trouble. If the product has outlived its usefulness, or been replaced by new technologies, it should be abandoned.

1.11 Situation Analysis Summary.

The information that you have compiled is a complete picture of your present position. You should now know:

1. Your customers and their needs
2. Your strengths and weaknesses in meeting these needs
3. Your position in the market
4. Your competitors' positions

With this information, you are now ready to prepare strategies and plans that will help you meet the goals of your property.

1.12 The Marketing Information System.

Before embarking on the Strategy section, it is important for your client to create a reliable Marketing Information System. A Marketing Information System (MIS) can range from a very simple collection of data to a complex, organization-wide commitment to research. In most small businesses, it will be easy to establish and maintain an MIS.

Marketing data is everywhere. Customer records, transaction reports, sales call reports, trade journals, and other sources are all full of marketing information. An MIS captures the information, sorts through it for pertinent data, summarizes the data in a meaningful way, and forms the basis for recommendations or strategies. This process is outlined in the following list:

1. Identify Information Needs
2. Identify Potential Sources
3. Establish a System For Capturing Information
4. Create Meaningful Summaries
5. Establish a Routine For Using Information
6. Evaluate the MIS

You can assist your client in all six steps. The following paragraphs will provide some guidance.

1. <u>Identify Information Needs</u>

The first step is to determine the information needs of the organization. Usually, information will not be used if no one requests it. Of course, many managers do not realize that they need additional data. They base their decisions on "feelings or guesses." As a consultant, you can provide a valuable service by determining your client's needs for information.

Information Needs can generally be divided into five categories. They are:

a.   Current Customer Information: This is data about the current customer base. This could include satisfaction levels, frequency of purchase, average purchase price, etc. This information can often be found in the current files of the organization. For example, to obtain the average purchase price, simply divide sales revenues by the number of items purchased.

b.   General Market Information: This would include industry trends, market growth or decline, etc. This information is often available from secondary sources such as trade magazines, government reports or consultant files. This data usually needs to be adjusted for current market conditions.

c.   Competitive Information: There are many ways to obtain this data. Remember, always operate in an ethical manner. In a proper MIS, quality information is developed in an ongoing basis -- without diminishing the integrity of the company.

d.   Environmental Information: This manual already provides some detail on the environmental information search. In an MIS, the information collection is formalized.

e.   Marketing Efficiency: Most managers would like to know if their marketing activities are beneficial. This can be an important part of the MIS. Each organization should make plans to evaluate and report on the progress of their plans.

2.   Identify Potential Sources

There are two types of information that are gathered in an MIS. Primary information is data that is created by or for the organization. Secondary information is generated for a broader market. For example, an analysis of Haggerty's current customers' average check at lunch could be performed using primary data from the lunch checks. However, information about the size of the local market might be obtained through state or local government reports. This is an example of secondary data.

When a marketer discovers a need for information, the very next step is to determine the location of that information. In many cases, a single marketing question could require several information sources, both secondary and primary.

3.   Establish A System For Capturing Information

When a systematic approach to any problem is established, it should create consistency. A systematic approach to data collection will require management to identify the person in charge, a time frame, and an evaluation process. If Haggerty's wanted to determine, on a monthly basis, the average guest check at lunch, they would need a system. Ms. Chelsea could appoint an assistant manager to collect the guest checks from a certain point each day. The manager would then use the office computer to make the calculations. Ms. Chelsea would evaluate the performance of the assistant manager.

Unless responsibility for data collection is specifically assigned, the information will probably not be located. A budget line may be necessary for subscription costs or for consultant's fees.

4.   Create Meaningful Summaries

Once the information has been gathered, it must be analyzed and summarized. This is best accomplished by placing regularly collected data in a standard format. By creating forms or reports, the information is presented in a consistent manner.

At Haggerty's, the marketing information is calculated and placed onto forms that are kept in an office folder. At the end of each month, the information is compiled into graphics and presented at the monthly management meeting. For examples of typical graphs and charts, please refer to Appendix 4A.

5.   Establish Routines For Using Data

It is certainly annoying when data is collected, collated, tabulated, and then ignored. As a student, you would be upset if your professor asked you to perform an assignment, then he/she never collected it. The same situation occurs in modern management on an all too frequent basis.

It is imperative to utilize, or at least review, the information that is collected. Encourage your client to set up a schedule for reading and discussing the information.

6.   Evaluate the MIS

Periodically, the MIS should be reviewed and evaluated. This should take two directions. First, the usefulness of each section of data should be evaluated. Second, the accuracy and completeness of all the information should be assessed.

Determining the usefulness should be easy, but the task is complicated by human nature. If someone's job is, to some degree, dependent upon compiling information, it will be difficult to eliminate it. However, by conscientiously applying step one (identify information needs) to all data it will quickly become apparent whether the data is important or not.

Accuracy of the information should be checked frequently. This could be done by an outside consultant. This lends impartiality to the proceedings. If another employee is used, the procedure should be discussed in advance.

Summary of the MIS Process

Creating an accurate and dependable MIS is very important for your client. If they have a system in place now, review it with them. Make certain that it conforms to the six steps outlined in this section.

If there is no MIS now, help your client create one. The forms contained in APPENDIX 6I should prove helpful. By establishing an accurate MIS, your client will benefit from your work long after the current Marketing Plan has been utilized.

APPENDIX 6A
CREATING A BENEFIT/SEGMENT MATRIX

Begin your matrix by identifying all the benefits of your product. (Remember to include the suggestions of your customers and co-workers.) You may wish to make copies of this form for future use.

PRODUCT: _____

BENEFITS:
1. _____
2. _____
3. _____
4. _____
5. _____
6. _____
7. _____

Now briefly describe the segments you feel would be interested in your product. Segments represent marketing opportunities. Next to the name of each segment, check whether the segment is growing, declining, or stabilizing in the appropriate column.

	SEGMENT	GROWING	DECLINING	STABILIZING
1.	_____	____	____	____
	_____			
2.	_____	____	____	____
	_____			
3.	_____	____	____	____
	_____			
4.	_____	____	____	____
	_____			
5.	_____	____	____	____
	_____			

List one benefit on each line provided beneath BENEFITS. List one segment on each line provided beneath SEGMENTS. Center an X between each benefit and segment that correspond.

SEGMENTS

1)_____ 2)_____ 3)_____ 4)_____ 5)_____

BENEFITS

1) _____

2) _____

3) _____

4) _____

5) _____

6) _____

7) _____

You now have a working Benefit/Segment Matrix. This should help you better define existing market segments, as well as identify new market segments.

APPENDIX 6B
PRICE/CONTRIBUTION ANALYSIS

In the spaces below, list each product that is offered by your client. Next to it, list the total variable costs for that product. If you are unable to determine the exact variable cost, make an estimate. Your client may be hesitant to share some of this information with you. Copy this form for more room.

Product _____ Selling Price _____

Variable Costs (Type and Dollar Value) _____

_____

_____

Contribution Margin _____

Product _____ Selling Price _____

Variable Costs (Type and Dollar Value) _____

_____

_____

Contribution Margin _____

Product _____ Selling Price _____

Variable Costs (Type and Dollar Value) _____

_____

_____

Contribution Margin _____

Product _____ Selling Price _____

Variable Costs (Type and Dollar Value) _____

_____

_____

Contribution Margin _____

Product _____ Selling Price _____

Variable Costs (Type and Dollar Value) _____

_____

_____

Contribution Margin _____

Product _____ Selling Price _____

Variable Costs (Type and Dollar Value) _____

_____

_____

Contribution Margin _____

Now, use the information above to calculate the total contribution margin for this company. For consistency, choose the same sales period for each product. For example, calculate the number of units sold for a certain week, month, etc.

Sales Mix Calculation
Sales Period _____ to _____

Product	Unit Contribution Margin	Number Sold	Total Contribution Margin
TOTAL			

APPENDIX 6C
ANALYZING PROMOTIONAL EFFECTIVENESS

Use the form below to rate the effectiveness of each promotion. Copy this form for more room. If you have some calculations to reinforce your evaluation, attach them to this form.

Promotion	Calculations Attached?		Success Rating Poor_____Good				
_____	Yes	No	1	2	3	4	5
_____	Yes	No	1	2	3	4	5
_____	Yes	No	1	2	3	4	5
_____	Yes	No	1	2	3	4	5
_____	Yes	No	1	2	3	4	5
_____	Yes	No	1	2	3	4	5
_____	Yes	No	1	2	3	4	5
_____	Yes	No	1	2	3	4	5
_____	Yes	No	1	2	3	4	5
_____	Yes	No	1	2	3	4	5
_____	Yes	No	1	2	3	4	5
_____	Yes	No	1	2	3	4	5
_____	Yes	No	1	2	3	4	5
_____	Yes	No	1	2	3	4	5
_____	Yes	No	1	2	3	4	5
_____	Yes	No	1	2	3	4	5
_____	Yes	No	1	2	3	4	5

APPENDIX 6D
ANALYZING YOUR COMPETITION

Use this form as a guide for analyzing the competition. Copy this form if you need more room.

Competitor: _____

Address: _____

Organization: _____

Parent company: _____

Subsidiaries: _____

Marketing Director: _____

His/Her experience: _____

Description of sales organization: _____

_____

_____

Product name and description: _____

_____

_____

Sales history: _____

_____

Recent changes in the product: _____

_____

Price structures: _____

_____

Distribution: _____

_____

Types of promotions and probable costs: _____

_____

_____

Description of the market segments the competition serves: _____

_____

_____

Most outstanding benefits the product offers these segments: _____

_____

_____

Weaknesses of the product in relation to these segments: _____

_____

_____

How their product compares with yours: _____

_____

Where is this competitor placed on the Benefit/Segment Matrix? _____

_____

_____

Major strategy for competing with this product: _____

_____

_____

APPENDIX 6E
SEGMENTING THE MARKET

Carefully write in all information gathered on each segment. Be specific. You may wish to make copies of this form for extra room.

Primary segment: _____

Demographic variables common to this segment: _____

_____

Geographic origins: _____

_____

Usage-rate and other usage features: _____

_____

Secondary segment: _____

Demographic variables common to this segment: _____

_____

Geographic origins: _____

_____

Usage-rate and other usage features: _____

_____

Tertiary segment: _____

Demographic variables common to this segment: _____

_____

Geographic origins: _____

_____

Usage-rate and other usage features: _____

_____

APPENDIX 6F
PREDICTING MARKET GROWTH OR DECLINE

Use the following list as a log for cataloging the information that you hope to acquire. Make copies of this form for more room.

Market Segment _____

Type of Information Needed   Source of Information
to Predict Growth or Decline

_____   _____

_____   _____

_____   _____

_____   _____

_____   _____

_____   _____

_____   _____

_____   _____

_____   _____

_____   _____

_____   _____

_____   _____

_____   _____

_____   _____

_____   _____

_____   _____

APPENDIX 6G
THE MARKET ENVIRONMENT

Use the spaces below to carefully analyze the environmental variables that affect your client. Start with the most obvious conditions first and then proceed to the more subtle variables. After listing each environmental influence, list the opportunities or challenges that each presents. Make copies of this form if you need more room.

Legal

1.   Variable _____

        Opportunity/Challenge _____

        _____

2.   Variable _____

        Opportunity/Challenge _____

        _____

3.   Variable _____

        Opportunity/Challenge _____

        _____

4.   Variable _____

        Opportunity/Challenge _____

        _____

5.   Variable _____

        Opportunity/Challenge _____

        _____

Political

1.   Variable _____

        Opportunity/Challenge _____

        _____

2.   Variable _____

        Opportunity/Challenge _____

        _____

3.   Variable _____

        Opportunity/Challenge _____

        _____

4.   Variable _____

       Opportunity/Challenge   _____

       _____

5.   Variable _____

       Opportunity/Challenge   _____

       _____

Technological

1.   Variable _____

       Opportunity/Challenge   _____

       _____

2.   Variable _____

       Opportunity/Challenge   _____

       _____

3.   Variable _____

       Opportunity/Challenge   _____

       _____

4.   Variable _____

       Opportunity/Challenge   _____

       _____

5.   Variable _____

       Opportunity/Challenge   _____

       _____

Social

1.   Variable _____

       Opportunity/Challenge   _____

       _____

2.   Variable _____

       Opportunity/Challenge   _____

       _____

3.   Variable _____

        Opportunity/Challenge   _____

        _____

4.   Variable _____

        Opportunity/Challenge   _____

        _____

5.   Variable _____

        Opportunity/Challenge   _____

        _____

Economic

1.   Variable _____

        Opportunity/Challenge   _____

        _____

2.   Variable _____

        Opportunity/Challenge   _____

        _____

3.   Variable _____

        Opportunity/Challenge   _____

        _____

4.   Variable _____

        Opportunity/Challenge   _____

        _____

5.   Variable _____

        Opportunity/Challenge   _____

        _____

APPENDIX 6H
THE MARKETING STRATEGY GRID

On the grid below, place your client's company and the competition. Then, list the reasons for your decision.

		MARKET DEMAND		
		Strong	Moderate	Weak
B E N E F I T S	Full	1	2	3
	Medium	4	5	6
	Limited	7	8	9

Reasons for this placement: _____

_____

_____

_____

_____

_____

_____

_____

_____

_____

_____

_____

APPENDIX 6I
THE MARKETING INFORMATION SYSTEM

Use the forms that are contained in this Appendix to define your client's MIS. Please make copies of this form as needed.

Information needs and likely sources for that information: _____

_____

Information Category (Circle one):

    1.   Current Customer
    2.   General Market
    3.   Competitive
    4.   Environmental
    5.   Marketing Efficiency
    6.   Other: _____

Information Needed: _____

_____

Who Needs It? _____

_____

Why do these people need this information? _____

_____

Where can it be found?

    Source 1) _____
    Source 2) _____

Who is responsible for compiling it? _____

_____

When is it due? _____

_____

How should it be presented? (Circle one)

    1.   Graph or Chart
    2.   Report
    3.   Form
    4.   On its own

When should the data be reported? _____

_____

CHAPTER SEVEN
THE MARKETING STRATEGY

OVERVIEW

Now that you know where you are, it is possible to develop a directional statement. Draw upon the information in the Situation Analysis to prepare this statement. You are now in uncharted waters. It is time to turn creative, setting a proposal for change.

By this time, you are somewhat of an expert in your client's business. In fact, you may know more about the customers, competition, and environment that either you or the client thought was possible.

Now it is time to look ahead. Anyone can research existing facts. Only a real marketer can forecast trends and then act on them. You will want to position your product to meet the needs of tomorrow's customers.

STRATEGY AND THE COMPETITION

In recent years, several theories and books have been advanced on the warlike aspects of strategy in the marketplace. There are certainly many similarities. However, this is not war. You should not try to vanquish the competition. Rather, your aim is to improve the bottom line of your client. Many companies have suffered because they wished to overcome their competitors, instead of overcoming the barrier to sales.

Who cares if the competition makes money? As long as you meet the financial goals of your client, you have done your job. Actually, there is nothing worse than a competitor who is about to go out of business. Why? Because they always have a going out of business sale.

Competition is best accomplished by searching the market for opportunities. Identify customer groups who will respond well to your product. Search them out. Fill their needs. Be BETTER at what you do. That is the way to compete.

2.0   WHAT ARE STRATEGIES?

Strategies are broad, directional statements of purpose. They tell the company what it wants to do and where it wants to be; they are the company's market guides.

Increasing sales, introducing and repositioning products, entering and discovering new consumer segments, and overcoming consumer objections are all strategies that the company's concerted efforts strive to reach.

2.1   Major Strategy Statement.

In this section, you will write the strategy statement for your client. This should be a serious task, because it will set the direction for the entire marketing project.

A strategy is often difficult to develop. Most people write strategies that are too specific and insufficient as a directional statement. Strategies are guides for the marketing process and reflect the policies of the company, not procedures. Plans are procedures and should not be devised until strategies are well developed. Conversely, strategies should not contain the operational, detailed information found in the plans.

An Example of a Strategy

The best way to understand strategies is to see an example. Haggerty's has many segments. However, the manager hopes that you will concentrate this marketing plan on just a few. She asks that you prepare a Major Strategy for The Seniors, Local Business People, Singles and Couples. You will probably need a separate Strategy for each segment. Below is the Major Strategy Statement for the Local Business Segment.

"The Major Strategy for 1993 (1) is to reintroduce (2) Haggerty's Restaurant (3) to the Local Business Segment (4) and to position it as a casual dining and drinking establishment and as a full service location (5) for small meetings.

1) Establishes a time for the strategy.

2) Provides an action statement. In this case, "reintroduce" indicates that the product should be revitalized in that segment.

3) Describes the positioned product.

4) Establishes a target market.

5) Provides a positioning statement. This statement is derived from the Marketing Strategy Grid. It indicates the direction on the grid the company wishes to take.

Once you have written your Major Strategy Statement, write some relevance statements. These explain why you feel the strategy is relevant.

These relevance statements provide reinforcement for your strategy decisions. Later, when the strategy is evaluated, the relevance statements will be examined to clarify the rationale used to determine the strategy. This reduces speculation and second-guessing that lead to errors. Below are the Relevance Statements for Haggerty's.

This Strategy is relevant because:

1. The research demonstrates that there is a need for this type of establishment.

2. The Local Business segment is growing and this segment already uses Haggerty's.

3. The competition has failed to enter this market.

4. The competition does not have the meeting space available to serve the needs of this segment.

5. The members of this segment are also members of the Couples and Singles segments. If they become loyal users of Business meals, they can be converted to dinner and weekend dining.

Haggerty's staff now has two choices. They can either design some other strategies for reaching the other market segments, or they can add the words "and maintain our current position in all other market segments" to the Major Strategy Statement stated above. In the latter case, the staff is declaring a major push in this segment alone and making the decision to "hold the line" in other segments. In any case, all of the strategy decisions are based on information from the Situation Analysis. Marketers should be particularly aware of the Marketing Strategy Grid when creating strategies.

Appendix 7A contains a form for developing a strategy.

2.2   Objectives.

Objectives are specific statements that establish a target for performance. When you take your first job upon graduation, you will want your boss to establish objectives. In class, you want the objectives of any task to be specifically spelled out. Objectives let you know when the task is complete.

Clear objectives should describe the state of the business if the plan is successful.

The objectives for your company should be measurable, attainable, and timely. Objectives perform two functions:

1.   They specifically identify the end product of the marketing program.

2.   They provide benchmarks against which the performance of the property can be measured.

Haggerty's Objectives

The following are examples of some of the objectives for 1993:

1.   Increase the number of meetings that are held at the restaurant to 15 per month.

2.   Increase the number of lunches sold to an average of 150 per day, with an average lunch bill of $8 per person.

3.   Maintain an average of 4.5 out of 5 on the guest comment cards.

Notice that these objectives all meet the three criteria of timely, measurable, and attainable. The objectives are all to be met within a year. Also, the numerical nature lends itself to measurability. Finally, the objectives are not outlandish. In fact, the measure for success in objective 3 is simply to maintain the current rating.

The exercise in Appendix 7B will help you write objectives for your client.

2.3   The Basic Selling Idea.

The Basic Selling Idea (BSI) is a description of the benefits that the product offers to the user. Great, but what does that mean? Let's talk about the problems of selling and advertising products. That might provide some insight into the BSI and its design.

The Message and the Promotional Tools

If a company has six sales reps and also hires an advertising agency to write ad copy, they could have a dozen or more people selling the product. Each of those people views the product in a different way. So, they describe the product differently.

But the company has spent money and time developing a product that has a SINGLE IMAGE. However, with all of these people turning around, it is likely that the core message gets lost. So, the company creates a Basic Selling Idea. This is written down.

Now, when the advertiser creates a message, it should reflect the BSI. When a sales rep talks about the product, he/she uses the description found in the BSI. In other words, the message is consistent.

The Customer's Perspective

Of course, all of this quickly becomes irrelevant if the BSI is not written from the customer's perspective. What are the real benefits to the target audience of this product? That is the question to ask before writing the BSI.

Lite Beer again provides a good example. The original manufacturer thought that the benefit was "Low Calorie." Drinking this beer did not make you as fat. But Miller looked at the beer from the customer's perspective. They knew that their major target did not care about the beer guts they had. Instead, they wanted to drink more beer. They couldn't though, because they got too full.

Miller said "Lite is less filling, so you can drink more." The perfect answer to the customer's dilemma. The Basic Selling Idea stressed the needs of the consumer.

Writing a BSI

It is not easy to create a good Basic Selling Idea. The message must be strong, concise, and relevant. The words you use will be transformed into advertising copy by the agency, public relations material by the internal promotions staff, and trade show displays. Finally, the sales staff will carry collateral material and make presentations using the BSI as a foundation.

The exercises in Appendix 7C will help you to write the BSI. Don't expect to be satisfied with your first attempt. The language of promotions is poignant, sensitive, and somewhat dramatic.

An Example

Haggerty's might use the following BSI for their local business market.

The Basic Selling Idea is that Haggerty's Restaurant is a business hot spot that combines the old fashioned charm of a friendly tavern with the efficiency of a highly qualified staff to offer quality food in a relaxed but professional setting.

When the BSI is complete, it is appropriate to offer some supporting statements. Here are Haggerty's:

This is supported by the fact that:

1.   Haggerty's is already highly rated as a good restaurant for business people.

2.   The staff is trained to remember names and to meet the needs of this segment for fast yet elegant service.

3.   The meeting facilities are located close to the kitchen so that food can be delivered quickly.

4.   The kitchen staff is committed to providing notable cuisine at moderate prices.

The BSI and the supporting statements should summarize the company's approach to serving and selling their segment. Appendix 7C contains a series of exercises that will help you to write your BSI.

2.4   The Market: Sources Of Business.

This can be a difficult section to write. This is particularly true for students. It is tempting here to put a few numbers on paper and then go on to the less quantified sections. However, this would be a grave disservice to the client.

The purpose of this section is to describe the size and characteristics of the most important market segments. In this regard, it is much like Section 1.8, The Current Market. However, we are now PREDICTING the market forces rather than simply describing the status quo.

Calculating the Size of the Source of Business

Basically, there are four frameworks in which to describe the size of the sources of business. They are:

1. Total Market

2. Competitive

3. Internal

4. Combination

Total Market. In this framework, the size of the segment/source is compared to the market as a whole. For example, a women's clothing store could be interested in the non-working mothers segment. They might estimate that this segment has 1,000 members. Their total market area is made up of many segments, with a total market size of 20,000 potential buyers. Therefore, the non-working mothers segment would represent 5% of the total market (1,000 divided by 20,000).

Competitive. This system compares one market segment or one company's market to the total demand in the entire competitive marketplace. For example, if a dry cleaner operates in a market with four other competitors and estimates that all of the the local dry cleaners launder a total of 5,000 shirts per week for the Single Yuppie segment, then 5,000 is the total competitive market demand in this segment. If the dry cleaner launders 1,000 shirts per week for this segment, then they have 20% of that competition (1,000 divided by 5,000).

Internal. Suppose a restaurant serves 800 meals per day. If 200 of those meals are served to older couples, then this segment represents 25% of the business (200 divided by 800).

Combination. This approach combines two or more of the other methods.

Haggerty's Sources of Business

Ms. Chelsea currently uses a combination approach for describing the potential sources of business for her restaurant. For example, she shows the following calculations for the Local Families with Children Segment.

She estimates from prior research that there were 1,500 families living in her primary target area last year. To be a member of this segment, the family must live in a private residence and have at least one child under the age of 18.

In order to determine the number of people in this segment, she contacted the city zoning commission to determine the number of homes in the area. She learned that there were 4,500. She then contacted the local school board to identify the number of school age children that were registered in the district. There were 3,000. This meant that there were an average of two children per family (3,000 divided by 1,500). Also, families with children represented approximately 33% of the total market (1,500 divided by 4,500). This is a fairly broad assumption, but it is acceptable for this type of analysis.

She called the city offices and learned that 300 new permits were authorized this year for homes in this area. If 33% of them contain families with children, then 100 new families are in the market. This is an increase of about 6% (100 divided by 1,500).

She knows, from reading industry trade publications, that the average family with children eats .5 meals out per week. If there are now 1,600 families with four members each, then this means that there are 6,400 people in this market. If they eat .5 meals per week in a restaurant, then this equals 3,200 meals per week.

She wants to serve 200 dinners per night at the early bird special. She also has set objectives to serve 25% of those dinners to families. She estimates that 20% of the family members are under the age of 12 and therefore, will order from the Kiddie Menu. If there were 3,200 people in this segment, then 640 are under 12. This leaves 2,560 over the age of 12.

The Early Bird special is open 7 days per week. 200 meals per day, 7 days per week yields 1,400 Early Bird meals. 25% of this is 350 meals per week from this segment. This means that Haggerty's will have to penetrate this segment by about 13% (350 divided by 2,560).

Presenting Data

There are many ways to calculate the importance of each source of business. Also, there are many ways to graphically portray this information. Refer to Chapter 4 for some suggestions for graphs that can be used here.

Show all of your calculations. Next year, when the plan is updated and revised, you will know the procedures that were used before. Without the calculations, it might be difficult to understand your rationale for the predictions.

2.5 - 2.8 Marketing Mix Strategies.

Now that you have placed your company on the Marketing Strategy Grid, developed a Major Strategy Statement, and written a Basic Selling Idea, you can develop strategies for the marketing-mix variables, the controllable variables the marketer can influence. The strategies for the variables are general statements of direction.

There should be strategies for each segment and for each marketing mix variable. If Haggerty's develops a strategy section for both the Seniors market and the Local Business market, then they should have separate marketing mixes for each segment. Each marketing mix is developed using the following three criteria:

1.   The Marketing Strategy Grid. Once you have placed your company in a box, read the suggested strategies for that box. The suggested strategies are the basis of your company's tactics.

2.   The Major Strategy Statement. Analyze your statement. All strategies developed for the marketing-mix variables help implement the Major Strategy Statement.

3.   Basic Selling Idea. The marketing-mix variables focus on the BSI. The BSI is fundamental to success since it represents the product, the product's benefits, and the consumers' needs.

Haggerty's Marketing Mix Strategies

The following are excerpts from Haggerty's Marketing Mix Strategies:

2.5   Price.

Seniors - This is a very price-conscious segment. The food will be discounted at the Early Bird special. Also, the prices should be reasonable at all times to attract this segment. Discounting through the use of local newspaper advertisements will be very important.

Local Business - The lunch menu should have a wide range of prices. More expensive entrees will be purchased by those on expense accounts. The less expensive entrees will appeal to those on a limited budget. However, we are not competing with fast food chains and therefore, will stay away from very inexpensive items. Combination pricing should be used to add value to the meal. Salads should be coupled with sandwiches and soups to offer perceived value for a lower price.

2.6 Promotion.

Seniors - Coupons will be used in local papers. Special sales promotions should be considered that use coupons and two-for-one specials. These could be distributed through local churches and senior centers.

Local Business - Company newsletters often sell advertising space. Also, we should continue the Secretaries Club. Drive time radio spots are also a good promotional theme for this market.

2.7 Product.

Seniors Market - This market enjoys large portions of wholesome food. Therefore, Haggerty's will develop menu items that are filling. Also, these items will be plated so that they appear to be very large. The food will not be too spicy.

Local Business - Since this is primarily a lunch crowd, the menu items for this segment will concentrate on luncheons. This segment prefers light lunches. Also, speed is of the essence, so all lunch items should be easy to prepare and serve. Finally, since this segment is often entertaining clients at lunch, the food should be easy to eat.

2.8 Place (Distribution in Other Markets).

Seniors - It is important to maintain a neat appearance for this market. Also, lights, ramps, and other items that make the restaurant more accessible are vital. The emphasis this year will be in changing the parking lot layout to accommodate more cars near the entrance to the dining area. Seniors will not have to walk through the bar to go to the Early Bird special. Also, they will not have to compete for parking spaces with the Happy Hour trade.

Local Business - This trade has given Haggerty's very high scores on the comment cards for all of the questions related to Place. Our strategy this year is to maintain that rating by maintaining the appearance of the building.

Writing Your Strategies

Remember to keep all of the statements broad and general. Depending on the type of business that your represent, the fourth variable may be Distribution rather than Place.

The exercise in Appendix 7D will help you organize and write strategies.

APPENDIX 7A
WRITING YOUR STRATEGY

Write your major strategy statement, including all five parts discussed in <u>An Example of a Strategy</u>. Be brief and realistic. You can further develop your strategy later. You may wish to make copies of this form for future use.

Strategy: _____

_____

_____

Part 1: _____

Part 2: _____

Part 3: _____

Part 4: _____

Part 5: _____

Now write your relevance statements to support this strategy.

1: _____

_____

_____

2: _____

_____

_____

3: _____

_____

_____

4: _____

_____

_____

5: _____

_____

_____

APPENDIX 7B
SETTING OBJECTIVES

In the spaces below, establish some objectives for your company. Use this opportunity to demonstrate that each objective meets the three criteria: Measurable, Attainable, and Timely. Make copies of this form if you need more room.

Measurable. Goals that are quantitative are measurable. Make some notes about the types of measures used and where the information can be found.

Attainable. Use some of the Math of Marketing that you will learn from Chapter Nine of this book to demonstrate the ability to reach the objective.

Timely. If a goal has a time limit on it, it is timely. The system used below will require a time frame. It is not necessary to re-justify timeliness.

Objectives

Short-term (within 6 months)

1. Objective: _____

   _____

   Demonstrate ability to attain: _____

   _____

2. Objective: _____

   _____

   Demonstrate ability to attain: _____

   _____

3. Objective: _____

   _____

   Demonstrate ability to attain: _____

   _____

4. Objective: _____

   _____

   Demonstrate ability to attain: _____

   _____

5.   Objective: _____

_____

Demonstrate ability to attain:_____

_____

Mid-range (6 months to 18 months)

1.   Objective: _____

_____

Demonstrate ability to attain:_____

_____

2.   Objective: _____

_____

Demonstrate ability to attain:_____

_____

3.   Objective: _____

_____

Demonstrate ability to attain:_____

_____

4.   Objective: _____

_____

Demonstrate ability to attain:_____

_____

5.   Objective: _____

_____

Demonstrate ability to attain:_____

_____

Long-term (18 months to 3 years)

1.   Objective: _____

        _____

        Demonstrate ability to attain:_____

        _____

2.   Objective: _____

        _____

        Demonstrate ability to attain:_____

        _____

3.   Objective: _____

        _____

        Demonstrate ability to attain:_____

        _____

4.   Objective: _____

        _____

        Demonstrate ability to attain:_____

        _____

5.   Objective: _____

        _____

        Demonstrate ability to attain:_____

        _____

APPENDIX 7C
WRITING THE BASIC SELLING IDEA

<u>Step 1: Assessing User Needs.</u> In the Benefit/Segment Matrix section, you examined your segments' needs. Your list of benefits should fit these needs.

List the needs of your segments, based on true needs, not your perception of their needs. Do not make assumptions. Ask your customers what they want in a product like yours. You may wish to make copies of this form for more room.

Primary segment name: _____

Unfulfilled needs:

1. _____

2. _____

3. _____

Secondary segment name: _____

Unfulfilled needs:

1. _____

2. _____

3. _____

Tertiary segment name: _____

Unfulfilled needs:

1. _____

2. _____

3. _____

<u>Step 2: Assessing Product Benefits.</u> Describe the benefits of your product that meet the needs of the segments. If the benefits do not fit the needs, then something is wrong. Either redesign your product or redefine your segment.

Write the benefits of your product in the spaces below.

Primary segment name: _____

Benefits that fill needs:

1. _____

2. _____

3. _____

Secondary segment name: _____

Benefits that fill needs:

1. _____

2. _____

3. _____

Tertiary segment name: _____

Benefits that fill needs:

1. _____

2. _____

3. _____

The Language of Promotions

The words used in a BSI translate into advertisements. For this reason, they need to be carefully chosen. Use descriptive words that accurately translate a "feeling" into an "image" and convey a message to the user. The message should be "this product is perfect for you."

It is difficult to choose the right adjectives to convey your intended message. Try and describe what the product *does* for the customer, rather than just describing the product.

The Basic Selling Idea

Write your Basic Selling Idea below. It may take several attempts to create a satisfactory one. Test its validity by reading it to an objective individual, then asking he or she to describe the product.

_____

_____

_____

_____

Relevance Statements

Write several Relevance Statements below. Simply restate the unfulfilled needs of your segment(s) and the benefits your product supplies. Your BSI may need rewriting if your Relevance Statements fail to support it.

_____

_____

_____

APPENDIX 7D
WRITING YOUR MARKETING MIX STRATEGIES

Make copies of this form for each of the segments in your market. Then write in the name of the segment and briefly describe five strategies for each marketing mix variable for that segment.

SEGMENT NAME _____

Price Strategies:

1. _____

2. _____

3. _____

4. _____

5. _____

Product Strategies:

1. _____

2. _____

3. _____

4. _____

5. _____

Promotion Strategies:

1. _____

2. _____

3. _____

4. _____

5. _____

Distribution Strategies:

1. _____

2. _____

3. _____

4. _____

5. _____

CHAPTER EIGHT
MARKETING ACTION PLANS

OVERVIEW

Action Plans are the instructions for meeting goals. As the final step in completing a working marketing system, they are specific, thorough, and complete.

Marketing strategies inform the company of what it wants to do and where it wants to be; the Marketing Action Plans, as marketing blueprints, state how.

This chapter contains exercises to help you write your Marketing Action Plans.

3.0   ACTION PLANS

Now that you have a Situation Analysis and Marketing Strategies, you can write the Marketing Action Plans for reaching your objectives. Action Plans, unlike strategy statements, are very specific.

Action Plans are divided into four groups: product, price, promotion, and distribution. Each group deals with a marketing-mix variable and may need more than one Action Plan. For example, if you have several different strategies for your product, then you need one Action Plan for each strategy.

The Elements of the Action Plan. Every Action Plan devised should have the following elements:

- date and number
- title of the Action Plan
- person in charge
- objectives
- plan of action
- time frame
- cost
- method of evaluation

To ease the difficulty in writing a good, strong Action Plan, each element is described in detail. Only well-written, organized Action Plans succeed.

Date and Number

It is important to develop a system for tracking and managing Action Plans. The first step is to date the start of development. A date makes it easier to reference the Action Plan, determine the market perspective at the time of development, and assess the chronological development.

In addition, your Action Plan will need to be numbered. A number identifies the sequence in which the Action Plans were developed, and its marketing-mix variable group (e.g. number 300 is the promotion Action Plans, number 200, the price Action Plans, etc.).

Like dates, numbers help you get what you need fast. Instead of sifting through all of the product information in search of the promotion Action Plan to advertise in AAA's magazine, for example, you would know that the 300's are the promotion Action Plans, and that number 309 is the promotion Action Plan for AAA advertising. In a minute, you can locate the promotion Action Plan by finding number 309. Simple.

Title of the Action Plan

Name each Action Plan. A name restates the purpose and objectives. It aids conversational reference since it re-emphasizes the Action Plan's focus. Names are also typically easier to recall than numbers.

Person in Charge

This person is responsible for the Action Plan's outcome and is judged on the success or failure of that outcome. The Person In Charge should have the proper background and training, be aware of the objectives and the time frame, and must have sufficient authority to obtain necessary resources.

Objectives of the Action Plan

Action Plan objectives meet the same criteria as strategy objectives: measurable, time-oriented, and realistic.

Measurable. Measurable objectives allow evaluation. If the objectives are not met, but the Action Plan succeeds, the Action Plan is re-evaluated, and objectives are lowered for the next Action Plan period. Employees are evaluated by their ability or inability to reach specified objectives. Measurable objectives provide a goal to strive for, such as 10% increase or $5,000 per week profit. If the goal is easily met, with little effort, then a higher goal can be set.

Time-oriented. This further defines objectives and goals and your success or failure in reaching them. Without time deadlines, prioritizing work activities is difficult, and objectives are not likely to be met.

Realistic. Realism makes objectives attainable. Goals set too high are never met, creating an atmosphere of frustration for employees and the marketer, sabotaging productivity.

Plan of Action (POA)

The POA contains step-by-step instructions for reaching your objectives and completing your Action Plan. It contains addresses, phone numbers, resource locations and rates, appointments, and location-schedules. Although the POA is often developed by the marketer, it should always be designed for the employees; they make it work. Therefore, the POA is specific and as "fool-proof" as possible.

Perhaps you have purchased an item that needs assembling. The instructions say "Easy to Assemble." Two hours later, after realizing you don't own the right tools, guessing at garbled instructions, and getting the headache of a lifetime, you are left with a product that doesn't work properly. Time, energy, and money are wasted. Avoiding waste is the underlying premise of the Plan of Action.

Time Frame

The time frame refers to the completion of the Action Plan, not attainment of the objectives.

Cost

The expected or projected cost serves as the Action Plan's budget. When costs of all of the Action Plans are added, you have a budget to work within. If the cost is too high and your budget too low, then re-evaluation, cutting or revising weak Action Plans or acquiring new resources may be in order. In addition, cost is the platform for other calculations.

When the cost of the Action Plan is compared to the expected outcome, a realistic assessment of the Action Plan's effectiveness is attained. For example, if the goal is to increase sales by 10%, with previous sales equaling $10,000, the answer is a $1,000 increase. If the profit margin is 40% (meaning the cost of increasing sales by 10% eats up 60% of the estimated $1,000), then the company stands to make a profit of $400.

Of course, Action Plans cannot be measured entirely on the cost basis. Sometimes it is feasible to make a market decision, regardless of the cost. If a competitor has a major advertising campaign that is quickly eroding your business, your company may need to compete to maintain market share.

Method of Evaluation

The method of evaluation is goal-specific. It measures the effectiveness of the Action Plan through the success or failure to meet stated objectives.

A Sample Plan. Although Ms. Chelsea did not have solid Action Plans written for Haggerty's, she did have some notes that she used to guide her marketing actions. The following Action Plan is an adaptation of those notes. When she saw a REAL Action Plan, she was amazed at how much detail it contained. She also admitted that it would make her job easier. "With this type of Action Plan, I could hold someone responsible for its success or failure. Before, I would ask someone to do something and I never knew what they would come up with."

Use the following Action Plan as a guide for your client's needs. An exercise to help you write Action Plans is contained in Appendix 8A.

1994 PROMOTION PLAN
PUSH THE PASTA PLEASE!

<u>Plan #</u>: 377

<u>Date</u>: 8/5/93

<u>Person In Charge</u>: Charles Harrison, Head Waiter

<u>Objectives</u>:

1.   To increase the per person contribution margin from the Early Bird Special by $.25 per person.

2.   To maintain the average number of patrons at the Early Bird at 120 per night.

3.   To provide both an incentive for the waiters and a means of measuring their sales effectiveness.

<u>Plan of Action</u>:

The new Early Bird menu features four dishes. (See PRODUCT PLAN #133.) They are:

TABLE 8.1
NEW EARLY BIRD MENU

Item	Selling Price	Cost	Contribution Margin	# Sold Per Day	Total Contribution Margin
Chicken Haggerty	$6.00	$3.00	$3.00	40	$120
Steak Jeannine	7.50	4.00	3.50	20	70
Seafood Surprise	7.50	3.50	4.00	30	120
Pasta, Pasta, Pasta	6.50	2.00	4.50	30	135
TOTAL				120	$445

This plan will attempt to increase the contribution margin by changing the percentage of pasta dishes that are ordered.

Presently, the total contribution margin per day from the Early Bird Special is $445. With an average of 120 meals sold per day, this gives a contribution margin per person of about $3.70. If this plan is successful, it will raise the per person contribution margin by $.25 to $3.95 per person. At 120 servings per day, this is an increase of $30 per day or about $900 per month! This is an important plan for us.

Steps in the Plan:

1. All of the waiters and waitresses will be brought in for a one-time, two-hour training session. The session will concentrate on the quality and history of pasta, its nutritional value and the exact ingredients of our pasta dish.

   Charles Harrison will conduct the session as part of his regular duties. Each waiter will be paid for their time. With 20 servers at $5.00 per hour, the cost will be about $200 for the two-hour session.

2. The chef will prepare sample dishes of the pasta for all of the waiters to taste. The cost of these samples is about $50.

3. Special promotional pieces will be developed to support this plan. Specifically, this will include table tents (plan #311), posters (plan #312), and special invitation cards to be handed to each guest (plan #313). The total one-time cost for printing these materials is estimated to be $1,000.

4. The chef will complete the development of the new "Three Pasta Elegante" dish (product plan #177).

5. At the end of each evening, the servers will present their guest checks to the manager on duty, who will record the number of pasta dishes sold. The record book is to be kept in the top drawer of the desk in Ms. Chelsea's office.

6. Ms. Chelsea will tally the sales for each server and present the information to the accountant at the time the payroll information is calculated. The bonus -- to be paid in cash -- will be in the pay envelope of each server.

7. A ledger will be posted in the servers' station that clearly tracks the progress of each server in selling the pasta dish.

8. To qualify for the award, each server must sell at least 40 pasta dishes per week.

9.   Prizes will be awarded twice per month, to coincide with the paychecks. The top pasta pusher will receive an extra $50 and the second place pusher will receive $25. Since there are two pay periods per month, this will result in a cost of $150 per month in cash prizes.

We predict that the new contribution margin scale will be as follows:

TABLE 8.2
NEW CONTRIBUTION MARGIN

Item	Selling Price	Cost	Contribution Margin	# Sold Per Day	Total Contribution Margin
Chicken Haggerty	$6.00	$3.00	$3.00	20	$ 60
Steak Jeannine	7.50	4.00	3.50	20	70
Seafood Surprise	7.50	3.50	4.00	20	80
Pasta, Pasta, Pasta	6.50	2.00	4.50	60	270
TOTAL				120	$480

If the predictions that are shown in the table above are met, then the plan will exceed the objectives. The new contribution margin per person will be about $4.00 per person ($480 divided by 120 people). The additional contribution margin of $.30 per person, times 120 people yields an additional $36 per day, or approximately $1,080 per month.

Cost of Plan:

The one-time, initial costs are as follows:

Printing	$1,000
Training	200
Food	50
Total	$1,250

In addition, $150 in bonuses will be paid per month. This means that if the plan is successful, it will lose $320 the first month ($1400 - $1080) and will make a substantial profit after that.

<u>Time Frame:</u>

The plan will begin on January 1, 1994 and will run for 6 months. It will then be replaced by the summer special (Promotion Plan #344)

<u>Method of Evaluation:</u>

Each month, Ms. Chelsea will calculate the contribution margin for the Early Bird Special and compare it to the predicted averages shown above.

3.1   Establishing the Marketing Budget.

Once you have written the Action Plans, it is possible to prepare the Marketing Budget. The Marketing Budget, like all budgets, should have three columns. These columns are: Predicted, Actual, and Variance. It is unlikely that you will be able to complete the entire marketing budget in your project. For example, you will be writing Action Plans that will not be used until well after your project has been graded. However, you can at least give your client the beginnings of a marketing budget. This will prove very valuable to them.

The Predicted column of the budget is used for the projected costs of each action plan. The form for the budget is contained in Appendix 8B. You will notice that there are a number of rows for Action Plan cost entries. In addition, we have included space for overhead costs. In some organizations, a portion of office supplies are charged to marketing. Also, office space and office equipment may be charged to the marketing department. Finally, staff costs should be allocated as needed. This will give a realistic projection of the total costs of the marketing effort.

The Actual column can only be completed at the end of the marketing period. So, for example, the budget could extend for one year. At the end of the year, the actual costs for each of the plans and other expenses will be entered.

When the actual column has been completed, the variance can be calculated by subtracting the actual cost from the projected cost. If there is a negative number, the actual costs were higher than the projected costs. If the number is positive, the actual costs were lower than the projected costs.

The initial reaction to a positive number is satisfaction. However, it may simply mean that the plan was not carried out properly. It is not possible to judge the success of an Action Plan on the budget alone. An evaluation form should be used to fully account for the success or failure of an Action Plan. A form for Action Plan evaluation is found in Appendix 8C.

While you will not have the opportunity to complete the entire budget form, fill in the Projected column. Then, show your client how to utilize the budget form at the end of the budget period.

3.2   Evaluating the Action Plans.

Your project will probably be over before the Action Plans are evaluated. However, you may evaluate Action Plans from last year's marketing plan. The form in Appendix 8C should prove very helpful.

Each Action Plan that you write will contain a "Method of Evaluation" section. This section will establish the routine that you will use to evaluate the success or failure of the Action Plan. Show your client the form when you submit your report. It should be filled out with all of the preliminary information. This would include the title and number, expected completion date, person in charge, etc. Then, when the Action Plan is complete, the client can fill out the rest of the Action Plan evaluation.

APPENDIX 8A
WRITING YOUR MARKETING ACTION PLAN

Reread your Marketing Mix Strategies, and choose one for this exercise (promotional strategies provide the most variety in Action Plan writing). Break your strategy into as many Action Plans as possible (one Action Plan for each marketing idea). Name each Action Plan and list its purposes to the right. You may wish to make copies of this form for future use.

Action Plans: Purposes:

_____   _____

_____   _____

_____   _____

_____   _____

_____   _____

_____   _____

_____   _____

_____   _____

_____   _____

_____   _____

_____   _____

_____   _____

_____   _____

_____   _____

Action Plans:

_____

_____

_____

_____

_____

_____

_____

_____

_____

_____

_____

_____

_____

_____

_____

_____

_____

_____

_____

Purposes:

_____

_____

_____

_____

_____

_____

_____

_____

_____

_____

_____

_____

_____

_____

_____

_____

_____

_____

_____

Now select an Action Plan from those you have listed. Review the eight essential ingredients described in Elements of the Action Plan to get started.

Action Plan Number: _____

Date: _____

Title: _____

Person in Charge: _____

Qualifications: _____

Objective: _____

Plan of Action (outline in steps):

1. _____

2. _____

3. _____

4. _____

5. _____

6. _____

7. _____

8. _____

9. _____

10. _____

Estimated Cost (show calculations):

_____

_____

_____

_____

_____

_____

Method of Evaluation:

_____

_____

_____

APPENDIX 8B
A MARKETING BUDGET FORM

PLAN NUMBER OR NAME	PROJECTED	ACTUAL	VARIANCE
OTHER EXPENSES			
STAFF			
OVERHEAD			
SUPPLIES			
OTHER ( )			
OTHER ( )			
TOTAL			

APPENDIX 8C
ACTION PLAN EVALUATION FORM

Use this form to evaluate each success or failure of the Action Plan. Make copies of this form if you need more room.

Plan Number _____

Plan Name _____

Person in Charge _____

Evaluator _____

Expected Completion Date of This Action Plan _____

Actual Completion Date of This Action Plan _____

Were They Met? (Circle One)   Yes   No

Objectives of the Action Plan _____
_____
_____

How was Success or Failure evaluated? State criteria and show calculations: _____
_____
_____
_____

Action Plan Costs

Predicted	Actual	Difference
_____	_____	_____
_____	_____	_____
_____	_____	_____
_____	_____	_____

Reasons for Cost Difference _____
_____

Overall Evaluation Of Plan (Circle One)

    Excellent   Very Good   Average   Poor   Terrible

_____   _____   _____   _____
Signature of Evaluator   Date   Signature of Person in Charge   Date

Congratulations! You did it. You finished the workbook and are now ready to write your own Three-Part System. This should be a relatively easy task, since you already have a head-start on gathering the information you need from the completed exercises.

Remember that the System, as your guide for working with a fluctuating marketplace, changing market trends, revolving competition, and transitional consumer segments, is dynamic and must be re-evaluated and revised periodically. Once a System is written and initiated, many businesses make the mistake of filing it away, only to be retrieved a year later, when revisions are many. This is unproductive. A highly prosperous system depends upon constant updating and adjustments to maintain a competitive edge.

Use your Action Plan as a handbook: measure progress on a monthly scale; determine the effectiveness of promotions; evaluate employees' productivity by their ability or inability to reach pre-stated objectives. With a thorough system, you will find that problems are few and success is plenty.

CHAPTER NINE
MARKETING MATH

INTRODUCTION

If you have already read this manual, you will know that Marketing is not just creative advertising. It is an attempt to generate income for an organization by increasing the sales volume or the profit margin. Market predictions are dependent on mathematics. Cost calculations are based on simple math principles.

In this chapter you will learn some of the fundamental formulas for market calculations. Most of them are very simple. Despite this, I have seen many students break out in a cold sweat whenever math is mentioned. If you can add, subtract, multiply, and divide, you are capable of mastering these concepts. So relax, just use your head and keep your cool!

THE FORMULAS

We will cover five formulas in this chapter. They are:

1. Weighted Averages
2. Contribution Margin
3. Market Growth or Decline
4. Sales Mix Calculations
5. Break Even Calculations

Weighted Averages. Weighted averages are used when one number has a proportionally higher effect on the average than another number does. While this may sound complicated, it is not.

For example, if your company sold three products, the average selling price would be higher or lower depending upon the number of higher or lower priced items sold.

TABLE 9.1
WEIGHTED AVERAGE CONTRIBUTION MARGINS

Case A

Item	Number Sold	Selling Price	Total
A	10	$10	$ 100
B	20	20	400
C	20	25	500
TOTAL	50		$1000

Weighted Average Selling Price = $20 (1000/50)

Case B

Item	Number Sold	Selling Price	Total
A	20	$10	$200
B	20	20	400
C	10	25	250
TOTAL	50		$850

Weighted Average Selling Price = $17 (850/50)

In both cases, the number of units sold was 50. However, in Case B, the weighted average selling price was $3 less than in Case A. This is because a greater proportion of lower priced items were sold.

Weighted averages can be applied to a variety of market calculations. Contribution margins, revenues, program costs, and sales mixes all use weighted average calculations when there are more than two items.

All of these formulas and concepts can inter-relate. They all use the same simple math principles.

Contribution Margin. Contribution Margin is a very important concept. It is more important than the selling price because contribution margin is used to defray fixed costs and to enhance profit.

Contribution margin is calculated by subtracting variable costs from the selling price. For example, if a restaurant estimates that a steak dinner costs $3.00 for the steak, potato, and vegetable, and an additional $1.00 for preparation and service labor, then the variable costs are $4.00.

If the steak sells for $10.00, then the contribution margin is $6.00. This $6.00 is used to defray fixed costs and when they are covered, it contributes to profit.

In this case, the variable cost percentage would be 40%. This is calculated by dividing $4.00 in variable costs by the $10.00 selling price.

The percentage that is left, 60% is the contribution margin percentage.

Market Growth or Decline. In your Marketing Plan Project, you will be calculating the size of market segments. Also, you will want to determine the growth or decline in those segments over the life of the plan. This, in itself, is easy. However, it gets more complicated when the total market growth or decline is calculated, based on the weighted average change in the segments.

An Example

The lunch trade at Haggerty's is made up entirely of three segments. They are Local Business, Seniors, and Students. Each of these segments is well-defined by geographical regions. Ms. Chelsea conducts market research to determine the growth or decline in the number of people in each of these segments. Her results are as follows:

1. Local Business. Last year there were 4,000 people working in the area. Since that time, new office space has been developed. There are now 4,500 office workers within the geographic region served by Haggerty's.

2. Seniors. Recent trends in urban rezoning have reduced the number of Seniors in the area. The census has declined from 2,000 to 1,5000.

3. Students. A branch of a local University has expanded. Previously, enrollment at the University was 2,000. Now it is 2,500.

As a market planner, you would be interested in the growth or decline within the segments and also with the effect this will have on the market as a whole. The following table will illustrate this analysis.

TABLE 9.2
WEIGHTED AVERAGE GROWTH OR DECLINE OF A MARKET

	Year 1		Predicted Changes			Year 2	
Segment	(A) # in Segment	(B) % of Market (A/8000)	(C) # in Segment	(D) % of Market (C/A)	(E) Net Effect on Total Market (DxB)	(F) # in Segment (A+C)	(G) % of Market (F/8500)
Business	4,000	50	+500	+12.5	+6.25%	4,500	53.0
Seniors	2,000	25	-500	-25.0	-6.25%	1,500	17.6
Students	2,000	25	+500	+25.0	+6.25%	2,500	29.4
Total	8,000	100	+500	+12.5	+6.25%	8,500	100.0

Interpreting Table 9.2

Table 9.2 uses weighted averages to demonstrate the total market growth or decline. In this example, the three market segments represent 100% of the total market for lunch demand. Local Business is 50% of the market, Seniors and Students are each 25%.

Note that the Local Business market is predicted to grow by 500 people or 12.5% of the Local Business segment. Since the Local Business segment is 50% of the total market, the net weighted effect on the market as a whole is a 6.25% increase in the total market (.5 X .125).

The Senior segment declined by 500 people or 25% of the original size of the market segment. This also resulted in a 6.25% change on the total market. However, this effect was negative.

The Student market also had a 500 person increase. However, since the Student market only had 2,000 people in it originally, this a 25% increase in this market. This also produced a 6.25% positive effect on the total market (.25 X .25).

The new market size is 8,500 people. This is verified by multiplying the original market size (8,000) by the total weighted effect (+ 6.25%) for a net change of 500 people. When this net increase is added to the original market size (8,000), we predict a total of 8,500 people in year 2.

Using the Prediction

Probably the best use for the prediction is to calculate market penetration. If Haggerty's wants to serve 200 lunches per day, then they have to penetrate the market by some percentage. To calculate the percentage, divide the needed number of patrons (2000) by the total available demand (8,000). This produces a penetration of 2.5%.

In year 2, Haggerty's will require a smaller market penetration to achieve the same service goal. In year 2, there are 8,500 people in the market. In order to obtain 200 seats, they will need a penetration of 2.35%.

The market growth or decline analysis can also be used for penetration calculations that involve competitors. For example, if two competitors enter the market, the total market demand can be divided among all the competitors and then compared to the required penetration required by Haggerty's.

Sales Mix Calculations. Sales mix calculations are simply weighted averages that are applied to the ratio of products or services that are sold by a company. In fact, both contribution margin calculations and market growth or decline predictions can be a type of sales mix. Consider the information in Table 9.3.

TABLE 9.3
TWO SALES MIXES FOR HAGGERTY'S LUNCH PERIODS

SALES MIX #1				
Segment	Average Check	# Served Daily	% of Total	Total Dollar Value
Business	$8.00	100	50%	$ 800
Senior	6.00	50	25%	300
Student	5.00	50	25%	250
Total		200		$1,350

TABLE 9.3 (continued)
TWO SALES MIXES FOR HAGGERTY'S LUNCH PERIODS

SALES MIX #2				
Segment	Average Check	# Served Daily	% of Total	Total Dollar Value
Business	$8.00	80	40%	$ 640
Senior	6.00	50	25%	300
Student	5.00	70	35%	350
Total		200		$1,290

In sales mix #1, the total revenue from sales is $1,350. However, in sales mix #2, even though there are still 200 lunches served, the total revenue is only $1,290. The type of sales mix can certainly affect the profitability.

Of course, we believe that it is better to conduct a sales mix analysis by using contribution margins rather than selling price. We have used this example in the illustration of contribution margin calculations. However, many companies are unable to provide accurate variable cost information. For them, a simple sales mix analysis is best.

Break Even Calculations. Marketers use break even calculations to determine the level at which their marketing efforts can pay for the cost of the program. For example, if a company advertises a product, they would probably like to know how many products they have to sell to pay for the advertisement.

Break even analysis is based on the use of fixed costs, variable costs, and profit. Rather than simply giving you some formulas, we will use several examples to explain the marketer's use of break even analysis.

Example #1

A company has an overhead of $2,000 per week. They sell "units" for $50 each. It costs the company $25 per unit in variable costs. Answer the following questions:

    1.   What sales volume does this company need to break even?

    2.   How many units do they need to sell to break even?

Step 1. Calculate the variable cost percent:

          (Variable cost divided by selling price: $25/$50 = 50%)

Step 2. Use the break even formula to calculate the sales volume:

$$\frac{\text{Fixed Cost}}{1-\text{Variable Cost \%}} \quad = \quad \frac{\$2{,}000}{.5} \quad = \quad \$4{,}000$$

Step 3. Calculate the number of units that must be sold:

$$\frac{\text{Total Sales Needed}}{\text{Selling Price Per Unit}} \quad = \quad \frac{\$4{,}000}{\$50} \quad = \quad 80$$

Example #2

This same company wants to show a $3,000 profit per week. What sales volume do they need? How many units must they sell?

Step 1. Calculate the variable cost percent:

          (Variable cost divided by selling price: $25/$50 = 50%)

Step 2. Use the profit prediction formula to calculate the sales volume:

$$\frac{\text{Fixed Cost + Profit}}{1-\text{Variable Cost \%}} \quad = \quad \frac{\$2{,}000 + \$3{,}000}{.5} \quad = \quad \$10{,}000$$

Step 3. Calculate the number of units that must be sold:

$$\frac{\text{Total Revenue Needed}}{\text{Selling Price Per Unit}} \quad = \quad \frac{\$10,000}{50} \quad = \quad 200$$

Example #3

The company in the first two examples wishes to embark on an advertising campaign. The campaign will cost $6,000. How many additional units must this company sell to pay for the advertising?

In this case, the cost of the advertising becomes a fixed cost. So, the formulas are exactly the same. Selling price is still $50. Variable costs are still $25. Therefore, the variable cost percentage is still 50%.

$$\frac{\text{Cost of Advertising}}{\text{1-Variable Cost \%}} \quad = \quad \frac{\$6,000}{.5} \quad = \quad \$12,000$$

An additional $12,000 in sales is needed. How many units should be sold? Simple!

$$\frac{\text{Sales Volume Needed}}{\text{Selling Price Per Unit}} \quad = \quad \frac{\$12,000}{50} \quad = \quad 240$$

The company originally needed $10,000 in sales to reach a profit of $2,000. Then they decided to embark on an expensive advertising campaign. They now require an additional $12,000 in sales volume to pay for the advertising. They now require a total sales volume of $22,000 to both pay for the campaign and render a $2,000 profit. They must sell 330 total units to meet these needs.

Example #4

If this company operates in a market with 10,000 units of demand, they can calculate the penetration necessary to reach each of their goals. Consider:

1. To break even, the penetration necessary is .8% (80 units divided by 10,000 units).

2. The penetration needed to achieve a profit of $2,000 is 2% (200 units divided by 10,000 units).

3. The penetration needed to have a profit of $2,000 and to pay for a $6,000 advertising campaign is 4.4% (440 units divided by 10,000 units).

Summary of Marketing Math

The principles of mathematics as applied to marketing are relatively simple. You are certainly capable of using them.

It is important to be both creative and practical when producing a marketing plan. Creativity is evident in the Basic Selling Idea and the Strategies. Also, the Action Plans will depend upon your ability to look at the market process from the viewpoint of the consumer.

However, the needs of the organization must be met. Therefore, it is imperative that you are able to project the growth of segments, the contribution margin, and the break even or profit levels. You need mathematics to support your creative assertions.

This section should help you to serve your client better. Check your premonitions and assumptions by applying these analyses to them.